Caminante, son tus huellas
el camino, y nada más;
caminante, no hay camino,
se hace camino al andar.
Al andar se hace camino,
y al volver la vista atrás
se ve la senda que nunca
se ha de volver a pisar.
Caminante, no hay camino,
sino estelas en la mar.

CONTENTS

PREFACE

Both parts of the title of this collection require an explanation. The call for papers comprised a bare invitation for a contribution on Antonio Machado without any specification or limitation; in the event, however, the offerings focussed, without exception, on the poetry, hence the baldly descriptive sub-title. And as with so many gatherings of this kind, certain connections soon became evident, less obviously perhaps in the pages that follow than in the convivial and serious discussions that succeeded and surrounded these papers, delivered in the comfortable and unpretentious - aptly Machadian - setting of Dalrymple Hall in the West End of Glasgow. Among other things the reader will discern in these essays a constant dialogue between texts, to use a jargon-free phrase in keeping with the tone of the Conference. It was as though contributors were mindful of the line from 'Retrato' - 'Converso con el hombre que siempre va conmigo' - and our roles were those of eavesdroppers as well as participants. These 'conversations' ranged from the work of the Golden Age mystics (McDermott, Cardwell) to that of writers of other perspectives and cultures (Round, Stanton), while, on occasion, the dialogue is between the poet and himself (Ribbans, Walters).

What also emerged from our discussions was the realization that our freely-chosen tasks were to engage with Machado's work, not his life nor, pertinently, his death: the concluding essay by Edward Stanton, with its finely-judged notion of priorities, is a fitting summation of the collective viewpoint. We were observant about the sombre circumstances of why we had assembled; but, clearly, this was, in every sense of the word, a pretext, and we moved on. But to be true to the poet we could scarcely have acted otherwise. It would have been an unfortunate irony to have erected - whether by editorial dictat, collusion, or by the very nature of our papers - a monument to a poet who could speak almost dismissively of his craft as 'una fuerza útil' and who was allergic to the marble of baroque art.

In this connection, the quotation that forms the title of this volume can be seen as an antidote to rhetorical commemoration, with its promise of eventual oblivion as soberly entertained by Machado's traveller in the closing line of the *décima* from 'Proverbios y Cantares' in *Campos de Castilla*. Even the casual reader of Machado's poetry cannot fail to be struck by the obsessive recourse to the image of the journey. It is, though, not so much its frequency as its peculiar vividness that catches the eye. It is a metaphor that changes with the poet: from the *modernista* path through the woods and gardens of the late afternoon in *Soledades* to the poet's ramblings through the streets of Soria and the Castilian countryside in *Campos de Castilla*, to the desolate strolls as a widower in Baeza, and to the visionary and terrifying 'rayo de un camino', the path heralding an uncertain future, in 'Otro clima'.

In the *décima*, however, Machado ultimately abandons this symbol. The switch of image in the last line bespeaks a refusal to take refuge in past achievement. Not for Machado's traveller the consolation of the backward glance at the path stretching behind but, instead, the awareness of times and experiences utterly lost. For such a view the imprint is inappropriate; better, the momentary ripple on the surface of the sea when a vessel passes. But, for all the bleakness, this conception is not entirely negative. If the life envisaged here is not one of enduring accomplishment, then neither is it one of futile striving. What we are shown is the traveller as survivor, indefatigable through the very act of journeying. We may not imagine him happy, as Camus believed Sisyphus to be, but, at least, he shares that same steady lack of resentment and bitterness as expressed in Salvador Espriu's brief poem 'Sota la pluja': 'Sense recança miro/com el meu pas s'esborra'.

What we offer, then, is not a monument, or even a homage, but with the sober example of the *décima* in mind a recognition that this poetry, open-ended and accessible, is still fresh and challenging. Like the more interesting journeys, it is an adventure with surprising and unexpected vistas. For helping to illuminate these features in the landscape of Machado's poetry the editor is happy to express his unbounded admiration to the contributors; and for bearing patiently with him through the long process to publication a no less grateful appreciation. In another of his poems on travelling Machado states that 'lo molesto es la llegada'; in the case of this enterprise, however, both the arrival and the journey have been a privilege and a pleasure.

Bearsden and Glasgow
April 1992

ACKNOWLEDGEMENTS

The editor is pleased to express his thanks for assistance to the following: Glasgow University Reprographic Services for printing the book; Nicholas Round for advice on editorial matters; Ann Round for assistance with the proof-reading; Christine Walters for the cover design; and, especially, to Isabelle Wood for helping to prepare the typescript.

BIBLIOGRAPHICAL NOTE

References to Machado's works are in the main taken from *Poesía y prosa*, ed. Oreste Macrí, 3 vols. (Madrid: Espasa-Calpe, 1989). Poetic quotations come from the second volume and appear in the form *PP*, 485; references to the third volume, which contains the bulk of Machado's prose writings, appear thus: *Poesía y prosa*, III, p. 1473.

The titles of the better-known periodicals are abbreviated in the form used by the compilers of the *Year's Work in Modern Language Studies*.

Songlines of the Dreamtime on a Map of Misreading (An Unscientific Meditation on the *Soledades* of Antonio Machado for the Evening of Palm Sunday 1989)[1]

PATRICIA McDERMOTT

University of Leeds

'Yo veo la poesía como un yunque de constante actividad espiritual, no como un taller de fórmulas dogmáticas revestidas de imágenes más o menos brillantes' wrote Machado in a letter to Unamuno in 1904 at a time of heart-searching over the nature of his poetic task.[2] The evolving Symbolist poet of *Soledades, galerías, otros poemas* could with even more reason be listed among the forerunners of what Yeats in his 1900 essay on 'The Symbolism of Poetry' had called 'the new sacred book, of which all the arts, as somebody has said, are beginning to dream'.[3] Yeats' question 'How can the arts overcome the slow dying of men's hearts that we call the progress of the world, and lay their hands upon men's heartstrings again, without becoming the garment of religion as in old times?' was a question very much after Machado's own heart, experiencing the same renaissance of idealism in the *fin de siècle* crisis of scientific rationalism.

Paradoxically it was the anti-scientific Nietzsche who in *The Joyful Wisdom* (an ironic appropriation of the *Gaya Scienza* of the mystical tradition) had proclaimed the death of God and with Him the death of all morality and idealism. He had ended his *Will to Power* with a description of the world in which the intrepid Superman of the future age would 'naturalize' himself: an endless (both neverending and pointless) cycle of creation and destruction of a monstrous force, the will to power.[4] But before man could realize his human nature, his will to power, he had one last battle to fight, and Nietzsche begins the Third Book of his *Joyful Wisdom* under the sub-title 'New Struggles': 'After Buddha was dead people showed his shadow for centuries afterwards in a cave, - an immense frightful shadow. God is dead: but as the human race is constituted, there will perhaps be caves for milleniums yet, in which people will show his shadow. - And we, we have still to overcome his shadow!'[5]

While Machado was happy to overcome the shadow of the Church (like the youngest son of Alvargonzález, to 'hang up the habit'), he was loathe to relinquish the shadow of God (like the youngest son, he did not want to kill the father to inherit the land - although in *Soledades* the shadow of Paradise is a feminine shade, a mother-image).[6] Machado was at heart an idealist engaged in a never-ending quest for transcendental illumination: 'Todos nuestros esfuerzos deben tender hacia la luz, hacia la conciencia', he writes in that same letter to Unamuno.[7]

The initial direction of that effort was inward, seeking, to use Saint Bernard's words, 'the defaced Image of God in Man'.[8] *Soledades* (1903) and *SGOP* (1907) constitute an increasingly conscious poetic examination of conscience and consciousness in which the three powers of the soul, memory, understanding and will, are exercised in search of knowledge of self and knowledge of God and a hoped-for identification and union between the two, i.e. the 'divinization' of man. *Sueño* and *soñar* are the terms associated with the visionary state and activity and the divination of spiritual truth. Whilst the poet is confident that he can achieve self-knowledge - 'Y podrás conocerte, recordando / del pasado soñar los turbios lienzos' -, his bet on divine knowledge is hedged;

> Tal vez la mano, en sueños,
> del sembrador de estrellas,
> hizo sonar la música olvidada
>   como una nota de la lira inmensa,
> y la ola humilde a nuestros labios vino
> de unas pocas palabras verdaderas. (*PP*, 487)

The echoes of Fray Luis de León (in 'la lira inmensa') and Santa Teresa (in 'la ola humilde... de unas pocas palabras verdaderas') are obvious and the poet appears to have been conscious of renewing the poetry of meditation and the mystical tradition, the tradition of an interior oratory that is at once highly personal and universal. Thomas à Kempis and Santa Teresa were major figures among the culture heroes and heroines of the group of Symbolist poets and latter-day mystics whom Richard Cardwell has dubbed the Helios Brotherhood, of which Antonio Machado was a founder member and which counted among its numbers some adepts of Theosophy, that curious glorious synchretism of Eastern and Western mystical and occult systems.[9] Like Yeats, Machado had access to their 'Divine Wisdom' and to such notions as the old Indian division of consciousness into the states of waking (jagrat), dream (svapna), sleep (susupti) and the consciousness of pure being (turiya), which seem roughly to correspond to the Western mystics' distinction between the states of meditation, contemplation, vision and union.

In *Soledades* and *SGOP* the poet retires into solitude for prayer and meditation (note the constant use of the verbs 'rezar' and 'meditar' and of nouns such as 'salmo' and 'plegaria'), making a spiritual retreat from historical time into the eternal 'dreamtime' of poetry in quest of ultimate reality. But even here the onward march of historical time is evident: although the poet would like to recapture the world-view of an age when faith was not incompatible with the accepted science, the view of a finite universe with God revealed in the signs of nature, he is

2

contaminated with the modern world-view of an infinite universe in which God is hidden or dead, the view of an age of loss of faith and collapse of meaning.

Where Santa Teresa´s silkworm cocoons release the white butterfly of the purified soul that ascends to union with the Divine, Machado's silkworms of suffering turn into black moths ('Eran ayer mis dolores', *PP*, 485).[10] The spirituality of belief, of ultimate certainty, is replaced by a spirituality of unbelief, of ultimate uncertainty. Unlike Chatwin's Aborigines, the men of the 'dream-time', who, with unerring homing instinct, follow the 'Footprints of the Ancestors' across the physical map of Australia, resinging their 'Songlines' with the same age-old words and rhythms, recalling into existence their original world-view and creation, the turn-of-the-century poet continually misses his way on the poetic spiritual map of Spain. Creatively 'misreading' the old songs and signs - in his 1931 prologue in the Diego anthology he quotes Santa Teresa, 'las "mesmas vivas aguas de la vida"' omitting the saint's identification 'que es Dios'[11] -, he 'deviates', losing himself in a labyrinth of uncertainty, going round and round in circles in a poetic landscape of ambivalence, with occasional tantalising, fleeting visions of the lost centre or 'home'.

The site of the memory of the lost paradise is momentarily revisited in the seventh poem of *Soledades* with its memorable introduction of the most important constant in Machado's poetic memory: the fountain and its associated lemon-tree in the patio of the house in Seville where he was born:

> El limonero lánguido suspende
> una pálida rama polvorienta
> sobre el encanto de la fuente limpia
> y allá en el fondo sueñan
> los frutos de oro...(*PP*, 432)

This description of the interior garden of childhood memory, a golden vision of the Great Chain of Being and Love, is a paradigm of the 'conciencia integral', unitary being which is lost in the Fall into consciousness, recorded in the last verse with the memory of the child-self shattering the reflected image and learning the lesson that appearance is not reality. Once out of the enchanted circle it is rationally impossible to get back in, but the adult does not give up heart-felt hope:

> y estoy solo, en el patio silencioso,
> buscando una ilusión cándida y vieja:
> alguna sombra sobre el blanco muro,
> algún recuerdo, en el pretil de piedra
> de la fuente dormido, o, en el aire,
> algún vagar de túnica ligera.

3

En el ambiente de la tarde flota
ese aroma de ausencia
que dice al alma luminosa: nunca,
y al corazón: espera.

Negative reason and positive intuition are the two 'modos de conciencia' in contention in the dialectic of rationalism and idealism which is the dynamic of Machado's spiritual and poetic activity, a dialectic which rarely (never?) finds a synthesis. And it is primarily in this failure to resolve spiritual conflict that Machado's modern poetry of meditation deviates from its Golden Age model. I quote Martz's general definition in his classic study of English seventeenth century religious poetry and its largely Spanish sources:

> ...a meditative poem is a work that creates an interior drama of the mind; this dramatic action is usually (though not always) created by some form of self-address, in which the mind grasps firmly a problem or situation deliberately evoked by the memory, brings it forward toward the full light of consciousness, and concludes with a moment of illumination, where the speaker's self has, for a time, found an answer to its conflicts. (330)

Missing from this concluding general definition is the specifically Christian religious dimension of the mental drama studied in the body of his text, and this is the area in which Machado often significantly deviates from his Golden Age ancestors.

Guided by Martz, a basic simple model of a meditation would be a 'composition of place' on which to focus the meditation, such as a scene from the Life/Passion/Death of our Lord or a scene from the natural creation ('the Creatures'), followed by an analysis and a resolution contained in a colloquy, whose frame of reference, whether in the form of a dialogue or a soliloquy, was always God or Christ, seen or unseen, the ultimate Presence. As Bousoño has pointed out in the case of San Juan de la Cruz,[12] there is an obvious kinship between the symbolic soulscapes of the religious and mystical poets and the Symbolist *paysage d'ame*, which in Machado's case is a fusion of traditional symbolic landscapes and personal life-settings (the garden of the soul and fount of origins / the patio in Seville; the highway or river of life / the byways and rivers of Castile). But in Machado's compositions of place, with their play of changing light and shade, the focus is on the life/death cycle in Nature, and in his colloquies (either soliloquies or dialogues with alter egos), the absence of the hidden or dead God/Christ is made more poignant by the echoes of the ghost voices of the religious and mystic poets of the past.

A case in point is the poem 'Yo voy soñando caminos', for me the quintessential poem of *Soledades*, with its song within a song imitating traditional folksong:

4

> "En el corazón tenía
> la espina de una pasión;
> logré arrancármela un día:
> ya no siento el corazón."
> ...
>
> Mi cantar vuelve a plañir:
> "Aguda espina dorada,
> quién te pudiera sentir
> en el corazón clavada."   *(PP,* 436)

Given the profane and sacred connotations of 'espina (clavada)' and 'pasión', I intuit, particularly in the context of the existential meditation which is the poem, that the experience of love referred to here is not merely human but divine. The poem is within the tradition of sacred parody, but it is an inverse Song of Songs, a lament for the absence of that love without which life has no meaning and the light of the way is extinguished. This is San Juan's Dark Night of the senses, Santa Teresa's state of Purgatory. Significantly Santa Teresa uses the image of 'espinas' for the trials of spiritual aridity, although the major image of both Teresa and Juan for the wound of the absence of divine love is the 'saeta', the very same image used to convey the sweet pain of the ecstatic experience of the infusion of divine love into the soul in the moment of mystical union.[13]

That Machado also experienced his moments of divine presence, expressed in terms of the flowering of a solitary hawthorn (a tree associated with both Christ and the Great Mother), is evidenced by a poem from 'Del camino':

> En la desnuda tierra del camino
> la hora florida brota,
> espino solitario,
> del valle humilde en la revuelta umbrosa.
>
> El salmo verdadero
> de tenue voz hoy torna
> al corazón, y al labio,
> la palabra quebrada y temblorosa.
>
> Mis viejos mares duermen; se apagaron
> sus espumas sonoras
> sobre la playa estéril. La tormenta
> camina lejos en la nube torva.
>
> Vuelve la paz al cielo;
> la brisa tutelar esparce aromas
> otra vez sobre el campo, aparece,
> en la bendita soledad, tu sombra. *(PP,* 444)[14]

In these two poems, as so often in *Soledades*, extremes of experience (if extreme is not too strong a word for a poet of understatement) are expressed in separate short poems, fragments in an aporetic text which brings together irreconcilable interpretations within a total structure based on the uncertainty principle. Longer poems often contain the contradictions within a single poem, microcosms of the macrocosm of the book.

A good example would be the eighteenth poem (*PP*, 441) with its explicit title 'El Poeta' and its overt biblical echoes, but I prefer to look at the thirteenth (*PP*, 437), considered by others to be the quintessential poem of *Soledades*, that other meditation on being and time and eternal destiny, resonant with a polyphony of voices from the past, whose structure bears a remarkable resemblance to the complex structure of an Ignatian spiritual exercise with its preludes and multiple points, colloquies and recollections of the composition of place. The poem opens with a composition of place, the first prelude in the Ignatian model, exercising particularly the mental senses of sight and sound, in the recreation of the spectacle of a summer sunset: apotheosis or twilight of the gods?

> Hacia un ocaso radiante
> caminaba el sol de estío,
> y era, entre nubes de fuego, una trompeta gigante,
> tras de los álamos verdes de las márgenes del río.

The image of the sun as a 'trompeta gigante', combining circle and music, suggests the harmony of the spheres, but also the Last Trump and Final Judgment, a call to a meditation on the Last Things, Death and Resurrection. The sound signals in the dusk chorus are evenly balanced: the light note of the cricket, the throb of life, Eros, the sombre note of the water-wheel, time passing, Thanatos. The word used for the sound of the water-music, 'son', however, indicates harmony and this is the nub of the first thought (note the emphasis on the verb 'pensar' throughout), the second prelude of the Ignatian model, the premeditation of the meditation, a forecast of the desired outcome: aesthetic emotion in response to the beauty and harmony of nature, an intimation of a divinity even if indifferent to man, cures the *angst* of the insignificant thinking man whose thought-process is both presumptuous and worthless:

> Y pensaba: "¡Hermosa tarde, nota de la lira inmensa
> toda desdén y armonía;
> hermosa tarde, tú curas la pobre melancolía
> de este rincón vanidoso, oscuro rincón que piensa!"[15]

Elsewhere I have considered this poem in relation to key *Pensées* of Pascal; here I would point to a contrapuntal relationship with key poems of Luis de León such as *Noche serena* ('Cuando contemplo el cielo'), *A Francisco Salinas* ('El aire se serena'), *De la vida del*

6

cielo ('Alma región luciente'), in which the contemplation of the night sky and the sound of music, whether human (Francisco Salinas) or divine (the Good Shepherd), transport the poet into an affirmation of the nature of heavenly bliss and a forecast of the Beatific Vision (the long chain of 'Entonces veré' in the poem addressed to Felipe Ruiz, 'Cuando será que pueda/libre de esta prisión volar al cielo').[16] But the moment of illumination does not persist in Machado's poem and the heart of darkness is plumbed before the meditation proper begins, divided into the ambiguous statement of the waters of the river, identified as a symbol of the soul (the detachment of the thinker emphasized by the explanatory parenthesis), and the ambiguous, unanswered question of the immersed poetic self:

> "Apenas desamarrada
> la pobre barca, viajero, del árbol de la ribera,
> se canta: no somos nada.
> Donde acaba el pobre río la inmensa mar nos espera."
> Bajo los ojos del puente pasaba el agua sombría.
> (Yo pensaba: ¡el alma mía!)
> Y me detuve un momento,
> en la tarde, a meditar...
> ¿Qué es esta gota en el viento
> que grita al mar: soy el mar?

In the first colloquy, is 'No somos nada' a nihilistic statement of the meaninglessness of human life, the absurdity of human existence, or is it the recognition of the lowliness of human life in relation to the grandeur of God, a necessary self-abasement leading to that humility which according to Santa Teresa is the foundation of self-knowledge and divine knowledge in the way to perfection?[17] Equally, the statement 'Donde acaba el pobre río la inmensa mar nos espera' opens out into a sea of monist and theist ambiguity: is it the Christian after-life of the conclusion of Jorge Manrique's *Coplas*, the cycle of reincarnations suggested by Machado's gloss on the same (*PP*, 470) - incidentally the last poem in the original *Soledades*: an endless cycle as in Nietzsche's Eternal Return or culminating in a Nirvanic state of bliss -, or the eternal union with the Divine of which the mystical marriage is a foretaste and which is described by Santa Teresa in terms of rain falling into rivers flowing into the sea?[18] The reader is not pointed in the direction of a single interpretation as in the eighteenth poem:

> Él sabe que un Dios más fuerte
> con la sustancia inmortal está jugando a la muerte,
> cual niño barbaro. Él piensa
> que ha de caer como rama que sobre las aguas flota,
> antes de perderse, gota
> de mar, en la mar inmensa.   (*PP*, 441)

In the thirteenth poem the question '¿Qué es esta gota en el viento/que grita al mar: soy el mar?' remains open, with echoes of the Romantic despair of Bécquer - 'gota de agua monótona que cae y cae sin cesar' - and the Theosophical affirmation of Darío - 'hay un alma en cada una de las gotas del mar'.[19] The *locus conclusus*, where one would expect a resolution, does not provide one. The conclusion of the meditation is inconclusive: the positively-charged sights and sounds (particularly the stars associated with the 'Noche de amor' in the eighteenth poem) multiply over two stanzas, but the scene is rounded off with the sound of the water in the buckets of the water-wheel:

> Sonaban los cangilones de la noria soñolienta.
> Bajo las ramas oscuras caer el agua se oía.

The circular structure of the poetic meditation serves to underscore the hermeneutic vicious circle of human reason and the limitations of natural philosophy in the attempt to penetrate the mystery of life/death/eternal destiny. *Docta ignorancia;* sense experience cannot be the basis for the religious knowledge; *Sapientia divina* is the result of the presence in the soul of a higher reality and its action upon the soul.

Santa Teresa distinguishes four grades of mental prayer: the first is that of unaided human reason and is subject to aridities and contradictions and is part of the experience of purgation - the soul thinks about God but does not know Him; the second, the prayer of quietude, is the first experience of supernatural prayer, when God comes to the rescue of the soul and illuminates her: this illumination is a free gift of God's goodness and comes unexpectedly to those who humble themselves; the third is a stage of increasing visionary illumination and partial union; the fourth is the culminating total union.

In her autobiography the Saint draws an analogy between the different kinds of prayer and different methods of irrigation, and the second degree, the prayer of quietude, the first experience of divine illumination, is likened to watering the garden of the soul with the aid of a 'noria'.[20] The Teresian source of Machado's 'noria' illuminates for me the interpretation of the poem which focusses on the waterwheel, 'La Noria' (*PP*, 460), the first in the section of 'Humorismos, fantasías y apuntes', a title which inevitably raises the question of irony in the interpretation of poems in this section. Here I part company with Predmore in his judgement that 'La Noria' represents an ironic commentary on the condition of man ('¡pobre mula vieja!') and the 'divine' poet who rules over his destiny in a section of negative, irreverent blasphemies.[21] In my view this central section swings between hope and despair, the two poles of the dialectic underpinning the structure of doubt built into the book as a whole, and I read (misread?) the poem as a divinely comic paradox in the mystical tradition, a rare instance of a resolution in the polysemic symbol of the waterwheel and its accompanying mule.

At first sight/reading the 'creature' who is the object of meditation, the mule turning the waterwheel, contained in the circular frame of the repeated couplet 'La tarde caía/ triste y polvorienta' appears to represent the poet/man on the treadmill of a pointless existence in time - '¡pobre mula vieja!' In the next stanza 'la eterna rueda' is an overt reference to Nietzsche, inventor of the eternal return according to Juan de Mairena.[22] Given that Nietzsche in the *Twilight of the Gods* had likened the philosopher to a tragic ass crushed by a burden he could neither bear nor throw off, and given the identification of the 'noria' with the thought-process in the final poem of this section, '¿Mi corazón se ha dormido?':

> Colmenares de mis sueños
> ya no labráis? ¿Está seca
> la noria del pensamiento,
> los cangilones vacíos,
> girando, de sombra llenos? *(PP, 471)*

the mule also appears to represent the mechanistic, rational, sterile thinker going round and round in blind circles, a prisoner of language eternally repeating itself.[23]

But the answering verse is open to the positive interpretation that the poet practised the 'prayers of the heart' which are very close to the mystical state, the 'prayer of simplicity' or of 'simple gaze', the 'prayer of silence':

> No, mi corazón no duerme.
> Está despierto, despierto.
> Ni duerme, ni sueña, mira,
> los claros ojos abiertos,
> señas lejanas y escucha
> a orillas del gran silencio.

In the mystical *via negativa* God is the Abyss, the Darkness, the Great Silence and in the colloquy of 'La Noria' the poetic self negates a negation to make an intuitive, 'heart-felt' act of faith in a Divinity whom he self-identifies as a Poet-Creator of a universe of harmony, whose divine wisdom and mercy is beyond human understanding and human language. The final stanza well illustrates Tillich's comment on this aspect of mystical experience: 'Language, under such impact, is beyond poverty and abundance. A few words become great words!'[24]

> Yo no sé qué noble,
> divino poeta,
> unió a la amargura
> de la eterna rueda
> la dulce armonía
> del agua que sueña
> y vendó tus ojos
> ¡pobre mula vieja!

9

> Mas sé que fue un noble,
> divino poeta,
> corazón maduro
> de sombra y de ciencia. (*PP*, 461)

The final nouns 'sombra' and 'ciencia' are an ironic challenge to the human negation of God made by Nietzsche in the *Gay Science* and an echo of the paradox employed by San Juan in his *Coplas hechas sobre una extasis de alta contemplación* with the 'estribillo' 'toda sciencia trascendiendo':

> Cuanto más alto se sube
> tanto menos entendía
> que es la tenebrosa nube
> que a la noche esclarecía;
> por eso quien la sabía
> queda siempre no sabiendo,
> toda sciencia trascendiendo.[25]

The heart breaks out of the vicious circle of human knowledge/negative reason and enters the integrated circuit of positive intuition/divine knowledge. Supernatural knowledge leads to a positive transvaluation of values - darkness is light, blindness is illumination, sterility is creativity. On a second reading, with divine insight, the mule is transformed into a symbol of the mystic visionary in communion with the divine, the wheel into a symbol of perfection, of heaven, its rotating perimeter presupposing an 'unmoving mover' in the centre.[26] On a second reading, the remarkable *tempo lento* of the *romancillo* in the initial composition of place, in rhythmic imitation of the movement of the waterwheel and the sound of its music, does not convey world-weariness but that trance-like state described by Yeats in his discussion of rhythm in his essay on symbolism in poetry: 'The purpose of rhythm, it has always seemed to me, is to prolong the moment of contemplation, the moment when we are both asleep and awake, which is the moment of creation, by hushing us with an alluring monotony, while it holds us waking by variety, to keep us in that state of perhaps real trance, in which the mind liberated from the pressure of the will is unfolded in symbols'.

'¡Pobre mula vieja!' The poetic subject identifies in cordial sympathy with the object of contemplation, the mule, feminine objective correlative of the soul, in the fusion of true contemplation. God is experienced within the creature who in the process overcomes her creatureliness: the derided mule becomes the king-bearer, an ironic counterfigure of the arrogant aristocratic Superman of Nietzsche.[27] Indeed the dialectic of this poem appears to be in ironic counterpoint to the dialectic of the Nietzschean 'revaluation' from *Human All-Too-Human* onwards, as described by Stern: '(1) A *description*, mostly hostile but immensely illuminating, of an accepted value or concept or personal trait forms the first stage (e.g. pity shames both the pitier and the pitied). (2) There follows a *rejection*, for reasons which are usually surprising and which derive from a projection of the original value beyond its usual range (pity strengthens the weak, destroys the strong; *ergo* destroys 'life'). (3) A *reinterpretation* of the original concept and an eloquent *acceptance* of it in its new form ('true' pity, making the strong aware of their strength, strengthens 'life').[28]

In my reading of 'La Noria', poetic compassion restores the traditional Christian virtues of pity and humility (Blessed are the meek... Blessed are the meciful...), and I am reminded of the second of the three degrees of truth of St. Bernard, corresponding to the three stages of meditation, contemplation and union: 'We rise to the first by humble effort, to the second by loving sympathy, to the third by enraptured vision'.[29] If 'Hacia un ocaso radiante' corresponds to the first degree of truth and prayer and 'La Noria' to the second, then the next-to-last poem of 'Humorismos', 'Anoche cuando dormía' (*PP*, 471) must surely correspond to the third, which Santa Teresa describes as 'un sueño de las potencias'.[30]

Another sacred parody of a traditional love song, this is Machado's most Teresian poem, its triad of images (fountain-beehive-sun) taken from the 'Moradas primeras' of the 'Castillo interior': the fount of grace, the bees labouring in the activity of self-knowledge, the sun of the light of the King whose abode is the centre of the castle.[31] In Santa Teresa's irrigation analogy 'enraptured vision' is the watering of the garden of the soul by God with the water of a river or a spring, but in relation to the fountain of the first stanza the unanswered question regarding its channel:

> Di: ¿por qué acequia escondida,
> agua, vienes hasta mí,
> manantial de nueva vida
> en donde nunca bebí?

also carries echoes of San Juan's *Cantar del alma que se huelga de conocer a Dios por fe*:

> Que bien sé yo la fonte que mana y corre,
> aunque es de noche.
> Aquella eterna fonte está escondida,
> que bien sé yo do tiene su manida,
> aunque es de noche.[32]

In spite of vicissitudes along the mystical way the Golden Age mystic poet is ultimately certain of his/her divine knowledge infused from without, but the conclusion of Machado's dream-song is enigmatic:

> Anoche cuando dormía

11

soñé, ¡bendita ilusión!,
que era Dios lo que tenía
dentro de mi corazón.

All depends on the interpretation of 'soñé' and 'ilusión'. The use of past tenses is not so crucial, as the experience is recalled in memory, and visionary experience is shortlived as Santa Teresa and others testify; she also warns that before the experience of mystical union proper, the visionary experience may appear to have been a dream or may even be the deceiving work of the devil.[33] Does '¡bendita ilusión!' in the *estribillo* reiterate the joyful possession of the vision of 'supernatural sleep' or the regretful rejection of the sleeping dream as a delusion in the waking state of rationality? Although the signs seem to indicate the latter ('manantial de nueva vida /en donde nunca bebí'), the reader cannot be sure.

The torture of self-doubt of the diabolical rational faculty in time out of dream is expressed in the poem 'Oh dime, nocha amiga, amada vieja', a self-dialogue which searches for an objective guarantee of the authenticity of the self-image and voice projected in the poetry. It is an inversion of the dialogue of the divine *Amada* and the human *amada* in the 'noche oscura' of mystical union: here both the *amado* (the creator) and the *amada* (the muse) are alter egos of the poet; there is no objective transcendental voice to grant certainty, there is only subjective uncertainty:

> ¡Oh! Yo no sé, dijo la noche, amado,
> yo no sé tu secreto,
> aunque he visto vagar ese, que dices
> desolado fantasma, por tu sueño.
> Yo me asomo a las almas cuando lloran
> y escucho su hondo rezo,
> humilde y solitario,
> ese que llamas salmo verdadero;
> pero en las hondas bóvedas del alma
> no sé si el llanto es una voz o un eco.
>   Para escuchar tu queja de tus labios
> yo te busqué en tu sueño,
> y allí te vi vagando en un borroso
> laberinto de espejos. (*PP*, 451)

The dangers of solipsism - that way madness lies! Machado appears to be referring to this in his 1904 letter to Unamuno: 'La belleza no está en el misterio, sino en el deseo de penetrarlo. Pero este camino es muy peligroso y puede llevarnos a hacer el caos en nosotros mismos si no caemos en la vanidad de crear sistemáticamente brumas que, en realidad, no existen, no deben existir'.

Machado's attempt to resolve the crisis of rationalism in mysticism was not a solution. He would attempt to solve the crisis of individualism by leaving behind the 'dreamtime' of the Symbolist world of *Soledades*, entering historical time and forging the poetic 'conscience of the race' in the poems of *Campos de Castilla*: 'No debemos crearnos un mundo aparte en que gozar fantástica y egoístamente de la contemplacón de nosotros mismos; no debemos huir de la vida para forjarnos una vida mejor, que sea estéril para los demás' (ibid.). Although Unamuno's influence was considerable in Machado's change of tack into active social engagement as a poet, the example of the active lives of his favourite Spanish mystics cannot be discounted. The meditation on the humanity of Christ led the mystic to works of charity and reform and Santa Teresa's 'que amor saca amor' finds an echo in Machado's piece of self-advice : 'la monedita del alma / se pierde si no se da'.[34] The 'affection' or will flowing out of the meditation of *Soledades* is the will to love and serve in the heterodox spiritual reformation of Spain.

Ironically, when he imitated the humanity of Christ in a poetic mission to his fellow Spaniards, he could not share the popular piety of his idealized *pueblo* nor its expression in the folksong he equally idealized. Unlike Santa Teresa Machado did not experience the consolation of the Cross in Seville;[35] his meditation on 'La saeta':

> ¿Quién me presta una escalera
> para subir al madero,
> para quitarle los clavos
> a Jesús el Nazareno? (*PP*, 558)

one of the *saetas populares* collected by his father 'Demófilo' in his uncritical folkstudy of the *saeta*, is a series of sorrowing lamentations based on a misreading.[36] The collective voice of the people identifies in compassion with the suffering humanity of Christ and wants to alleviate that suffering; the dissonant individual voice interprets a macabre and morbid ritual response to the dying Christ. The poet acknowledges his inability to resing the songlines of his ancestors (the change in metre highlights his spiritual divorce), his inability to recreate their vision, and ends with a defiant projection of an alternative spiritual vision in song of a living Christ walking on the waters of the unresolved (?) ambiguity of the eternal sea:

> ¡Cantar de la tierra mía,
> que echa flores
> al Jesús de la agonía,
> y es la fe de mis mayores!
> ¡Oh, no eres tú mi cantar!
> ¡No puedo cantar, ni quiero
> a ese Jesús del madero,
> sino al que anduvo en el mar!

NOTES

1   Inspired by reading Louis Martz, *The Poetry of Meditation* (New Haven and London: Yale University Press, 1971); Bruce Chatwin, *The Songlines* (London: Jonathan Cape, 1987); Harold Bloom, *The Anxiety of Influence* (Oxford: U.P., 1971) and *A Map of Misreading* (Oxford: U.P., 1975). As a hispanist-reader I feel 'the anxiety of influence' as I (mis)tread in the footsteps of innumerable Machadian masters such as Sánchez Barbudo, Gullón, Predmore and, above all, Geoffrey Ribbans to whom this paper is dedicated with affectionate gratitude.

2   *Poesía y prosa*, III, p. 1473.

3   Collected in *Ideas of Good and Evil* (1903) and reproduced by D. Lodge, *Twentieth Century Literary Criticism: A Reader* (London: Longman, 1986), pp. 28-34.

4   *The Will to Power*, translated by W. Kauffmann and R.J. Holingdale (New York: Viking Books, 1968).

5   *The Joyful Wisdom*, translated by T. Common (Edinburgh and London: T.N. Foulis, 1910), p. 108.

6   J. Herrero identifies the mother as the archetype of transcendental love. 'El sistema poético de la obra temprana de Antonio Machado', *CHA*, 304-07 (1975-76), 584-94.

7   In a biographical note sent to Juan Ramón Jiménez Machado wrote: 'Mi pensamiento está generalmente ocupado por lo que llama Kant conflictos de las ideas trascendentales y busco en la poesía un alivio a esta ingrata tarea. En el fondo soy un creyente en una realidad espiritual opuesta al mundo sensible.' *Poesía y prosa*, III, p. 1524.

8   Martz, p. 35.

9   See R. Cardwell, *Juan R. Jiménez: The Modernist Apprenticeship, 1985-1900* (Berlin: Colloquium Verlag, 1977) and my study '*Helios* revista del modernismo (1903-1904)', *Abaco*, 4 (1973), 55-150. A.F. Baker has studied Machado's thought in relation to Theosophy in *El pensamiento religioso y filosófico de Antonio Machado* (Seville: Servicio de Publicaciones del Excmo. Ayuntamiento, 1985). The major study of states of consciousness in Machado is S. Pérez Gago's monumental *Razón, 'sueño' y realidad en Antonio Machado* (Salamanca: Universidad de Salamanca, 1984).

1O   Santa Teresa de Jesús, *Castillo interior, o las moradas*, in *Obras completas*, ed. L. Santullano (Madrid: Aguilar, 1948), p. 406: '... y acaba este gusano, que es grande y feo, y sale del mismo apucho una mariposa blanca muy graciosa.' 'Eran ayer mis dolores' is the negation of 'Anoche cuando dormía' (*PP*, 471). G. Ribbans has revealed their publication within a fortnight of each other in February 1912 in *La Tribuna*, and postulated that they belong to a 'primer ciclo de Leonor'. 'Fe y desesperanza en dos poemas machadianos de 1912', *Insula*, nos. 506-07 (February-March 1989), 65-66.

11   Gerardo Diego, *Poesía española contemporánea* (Madrid: Taurus, 1959), p. 153. Santa Teresa, op.cit., p. 373.

12   'San Juan de la Cruz, poeta "contemporáneo"', in *Teoría de la expresión poética* (Madrid: Gredos, 1970), pp. 280-302. Bousoño compares Machado and San Juan in their use of symbol and in the sense of mystery, born of contradiction, that emanates from their verse. In his essay 'Sobre las imágenes en la lírica', Machado cites San Juan

14

as model in sparing use of imagery: 'En San Juan de la Cruz, acaso el más hondo lírico español, la metáfora nunca aparece sino cuando el sentir rebosa el cauce lógico, en momentos profundamente emotivos. "En la noche dichosa / en secreto, que nadie me veía, / sin otra luz ni guía / sino la que en el corazón ardía"'. (*Poesía y prosa*, III, p. 1211).

13   'Mas si es tierra que aún se está en la tierra, y con tantas espinas como yo al principio estaba', *Vida de Santa Teresa de Jesús*, in *Obras completas*, p. 100; 'sé que parece le llega a las entrañas esta pena, y que, cuando de ellas saca la saeta el que la hiere, verdaderamente parece que se las lleva tras sí, según el sentimiento de amor siente', *Castillo interior* (422). Cf. San Juan's description of the wound in the soul of the Bridegroom's absence: '... allende de otras muchas diferencias de visitas que Dios hace al alma, con que la llaga y levanta en amor, suele hacer unos escondidos toques de amor que a manera de saeta de fuego hieren y traspasan el alma y la dejan toda cauterizada con fuego de amor', *Cántico espiritual, Vida y obras de San Juan de la Cruz*, ed. Lucinio del SS Sacramento (Madrid: Biblioteca de Autores Cristianos, 1946), p. 921. Rafael Lapesa suggested Rosalía de Castro's 'Un-ha vez tiveu un cravo / cravado no corazón' as a possible source of Machado's image. *Insula*, nos. 100-01 (April 1954), 6.

14   Compare 'Desgarrada la nube; el arco iris' (*PP*, 473) and 'Acaso...' (*PP*, 464). The pattern of imagery of sterility and fertility in *SGOP* has been highlighted by M. Predmore in his magnificent article 'The Nostalgia for Paradise and the Dilemma of Solipsism in the Early Poetry of Antonio Machado', *RHM*, 38 (1975), 30-52.

15   G. Correa studies the lyre as a structural image and contrapuntal rhythms in '"Una lira inmensa": El ritmo de la muerte y la resurrección en la poesía de Antonio Machado', *Estudios sobre Antonio Machado*, ed. J. Angeles (Barcelona, Caracas, Mexico: Ariel, 1973), pp. 123-62.

16   See Fray Luis de León, *The Original Poems*, ed. E. Sarmiento (Manchester: University Press, 1953), pp.18, 10 and 27. In his note on 'La Ascensión' (p. 87) Sarmiento points to the Ignatian model in this poem. For the connection between contemplation and music and the application of the image of the Divine Musician to the Wisdom of God bringing all the elements of the universe into harmony, see T. O'Reilly's commentary on the 'Ode to Francisco Salinas' in *What's Past is Prologue. A Collection of Essays in Honour of L. J. Woodward* (Edinburgh: Scottish Academic Press, 1984), pp. 107-13. See Machado's 'Antología de Fray Luis de León para uso particular de un aprendiz poeta' (*Poesía y prosa*, III, pp. 1238-46). With respect to Pascalian thought, see my article 'Una meditación europea de origen sevillano' in *Antonio Machado Hoy. Actas del Congreso Internacional Conmemorativo del Cincuentario de la Muerte de Antonio Machado* (Seville: Ediciones Alfar, 1990), IV, pp. 125-38.

17   '... que la humildad siempre labra como la abeja en la colmena la miel, que sin esto todo va perdido...' (*Castillo interior*, p. 375). '... que es porque Dios es suma verdad, y la humildad es andar en verdad; que lo es muy grande no tener cosa buena de nosotros, sino la miseria y ser nada...' (p. 454).

18   'Acá es como si cayendo agua del cielo en un río o fuente, adonde queda hecho todo agua, que no podrán dividir ni apartar cuál es el agua del río, o lo que cayó del cielo; o como si un arroyico pequeño entra en la mar, no habrá remedio de apartarse...' (p. 463). In *Vida* (p. 121), Teresa ascribes to God infusing the grace of faith in the soul the words '"Mirad, que esto es una gota del mar grandísimo de bienes". For Jorge Manrique see F. López Estrada, 'Manrique, poeta del tiempo', *Los 'primitivos' de Manuel y Antonio Machado* (Madrid: CUPSA Editorial, 1977), pp. 179-206.

19 Bécquer, 'Hoy como ayer, mañana como hoy', *Rimas y otros poemas*, ed. Jorge Campos (Madrid: Alianza, 1979), p. 55. Rubén Darío, 'Coloquio de los centauros', *Prosas profanas*, 7th ed. (Madrid: Espasa-Calpe, 1972), p. 63. In 'Antonio Machado. The Poetics of Time', Robert Havard perceptively analyses 'Hacia un ocaso radiante' in terms of the Bergsonian opposition between quantitative and qualitative time in which the Pythagorean allusion with its echoes of Manrique and Luis de León gives a sense both of historicity and duration. *From Romanticism to Surrealism. Seven Spanish Poets* (Cardiff: University of Wales Press, 1988), pp. 86-91. One might add that with its multiple echoes 'Hacia un ocaso radiante' illustrates the vital poetic *durée*, the flow of literary history: 'Toda poesía es, en cierto modo, un palimpsesto' (*Poesía y prosa*, III, p. 1314).

20 'Paréceme a mí que se puede regar de cuatro maneras: o con sacar el agua de un pozo, que es a nuestro gran trabajo; o con noria y arcaduces, que se saca con un torno (yo lo he sacado algunas veces), es a menos trabajo que estotro, y sácase más agua; o de un río o arroyo; esto se riega muy mejor, que queda más harta la tierra de agua, y no se ha menester regar tan a menudo y es a menos trabajo mucho del hortelano; o con llover mucho, que lo riega el Señor sin trabajo ninguno nuestro, y es muy sin comparación mejor que todo lo que queda dicho' (*Vida*, p. 68). The plate (between pp. 368-69) by José de Orga for the 1752 edition illustrating the Way to Perfection shows Christ operating the waterwheel.

21 'The Nostalgia for Paradise', p. 47.

22 '(Nietzsche y Schopenhauer)', *Juan de Mairena, Obras, Poesía y prosa*, p. 510. The section of 'Humorismos...' is subtitled 'Los grandes inventos'. Machado's knowledge of Nietzsche is earlier and more extensive than that indicated by G. Sobejano, *Nietzsche en España* (Madrid: Gredos, 1967), pp. 419-30.

23 'Can an ass be tragic? - To be crushed by a burden one can neither bear nor throw off?... The case of the philosopher'. 'Maxims and Arrows', in *Twilight of the Idols*, transl. R.B. Hollingdale (Harmondsworth: Penguin Books, 1968), p. 23.

24 *Systematic Theology* (Welwyn: Nesbit, 1968), vol. III, p. 269, quoted in Colin Thompson, *The Poet and the Mystic. A Study of the Cántico Espiritual of San Juan de la Cruz* (Oxford: University Press, 1971), p. 154.

25 *Vida y obras*, p. 1244. For the influence of Dionysius's *via negativa* ('Unto this Darkness which is beyond light we pray that we may come, and may attain unto vision through loss of sight and knowledge, and that in ceasing thus to see or to know we may learn to know that which is beyond all perception and understanding (for this emptying of our faculties is true sight and knowledge)') on San Juan, see Thompson, *The Poet and the Mystic*, p. 8. Cf. the Bradaranyaka *Upanishad* (1, 3, 28), 'from non-being lead me to being, from darkness lead me to the light, from death lead me to immortality', quoted by M. Eliade, *The Two and the One* (London: Harvill Press, 1965), p. 27. Santa Teresa (*Castillo interior*, p. 459) speaking of the soul in partial union, draws a comparison with St. Paul in his conversion, blind and mute. The word 'mystic' comes from a Greek root meaning to 'close the eyes'. In relation to the apocryphal poetry see N.A. Newton, 'Structures of Cognition: Antonio Machado and the *Via Negativa*', *MLN*, 90 (1975), 231-51.

26 A. de Vries, *Dictionary of Symbols and Imagery* (Amsterdam/London: North Holland Publishing Company, 1974), p. 497.

27 A. de Vries (p. 331) cites as authority for the symbolism of the mule as 'king's mount' I Kings l. 33: Solomon riding on David's mule at his coronation (a pertinent association of wisdom and music in the context of this paper). Mule amulets are fertility charms and the mule's hoof is the only material not rotted by the Styx.

28   J.P. Stern, *Nietzsche* (Glasgow: Fontana/Collins, 1978), p. 105.

29   *The Twelve Degrees of Humility and Pride*, quoted by Martz, p. 16.

30   *Vida*, in *Obras completas*, p. 89.

31   *Castillo interior*, in *Obras completas*, p. 373. R. Alvárez Molina studies this poem as a 'conversión a lo humano' of Teresian language in 'Santa Teresa y Antonio Machado', *Cuadernos para Investigación de la Literatura Hispánica*, 5 (1983), 243-56.

32   *Vida y obras*, p. 1248.

33   'Dije que era cosa no soñada, porque en la morada que queda dicha, hasta que la experiencia es mucha, queda el alma dudosa de qué fué aquello: si se le antojó, si estaba dormida, si fué todo de Dios, si se transfiguró el demonio en Angel de luz' (*Castillo interior*, in *Obras completas*, p. 403).

34   *Vida*, in *Obras completas*, p. 121. Geoffrey Ribbans detects the influence of Unamuno here. 'Unamuno y Antonio Machado', *Niebla y soledad* (Madrid: Gredos, 1971). On the relationship of contemplation and action see Machado's confessional 'Retrato' in *Campos de Castilla*: 'Converso con el hombre que siempre va conmigo / ...que me enseñó el secreto de la filantropía' (*PP*, 492).

35   *Castillo interior*, in *Obras completas*, p. 434.

36   José María Abarbi and Antonio Machado Alvárez, *Las saetas* (1880), ed. V. Márquez (Cordoba: Ediciones Demófilo, 1982), p. 28

Antonio Machado, San Juan de la Cruz y el Neomisticismo

RICHARD A. CARDWELL

University of Nottingham

Decir que generalmente la crítica ha destacado varios temas obsesivos en la obra de Antonio Machado no es simplificar en exceso. Que el poeta sevillano se preocupó profundamente por el fluir temporal y las fuerzas destructoras que llevan todo a la aniquilación y la muerte ya ha sido reconocido ampliamente entre los estudiosos importantes. También su obsesión por el mundo onírico de los sueños y la memoria; también por una serie de preocupaciones existenciales incluso la cuestión de la sinceridad del artista. Lo que no se ha analizado con la atención debida es el tema, mejor dicho, emoción profunda, que es la ansiedad, neurosis que corre continuamente en lo que escribe Machado, sin excluir sus *Los complementarios* y *Juan de Mairena*. En verso tras verso de la obra temprana, especialmente, encontramos una serie de preguntas que expresan una profunda ansiedad. Añora 'un algo que pasa/ y que nunca llega' (*PP*, 434), habla de 'mi alegre leyenda olvidada' (*PP*, 432), se pregunta '¿Adónde el camino irá?' (*PP*, 436), '¿Dónde están los huertos floridos...?', '¿Al fin la alegría se acerca?' (*PP*, 459). Aun cuando el objeto deseado se le acerca, pregunta el poeta '¿Eres tú?' y continúa diciendo 'No eras tú a quien yo buscaba' (*PP*, 468). El imperfecto sugiere un proceso que nunca tendrá un término. Al mismo tiempo varios críticos han investigado toda una serie de 'fuentes' e 'influencias', particularmente Verlaine, Bécquer, Rosalía de Castro, Darío y varios simbolistas franceses. Así la poesía machadiana se ha visto como un largo proceso de ecos de un gran número de poetas precursores. Pero este proceso se complica cuando vemos que sus poesías tempranas forman una red estructural de citas y auto-citas, las últimas a veces irónicas. El poema 'Fantasía de una noche de abril' (*PP*, 465) por ejemplo, no crea, como ha sugerido G.W. Ribbans, una 'poesía narrativa [que] representa un esfuerzo de evocación de su nativa Andalucía - Sevilla, Granada, no especificada - poco frecuente en él';[1] más bien Machado crea una serie de citas y autocitas para inventar una parodia ingeniosa del modernismo romántico de la primera promoción (establecida por Jiménez y Villaespesa en 1900). Espronceda, Rueda, Villaespesa y otros modernistas andaluces son citados irónicamente a lo largo del poema, estas citas acompañadas por varias autocitas. El 'viejo salterio', 'la copla más suave' y especialmente los versos 'es el musgo que brota, y la hiedra/que lenta desgarra la tapia de piedra' hacen eco de otros poemas suyos, aun de varios versos descartados.[2] Este proceso de citar y autocitar ocurre dentro de una dimensión psicológica de una inquietud profunda. La poesía temprana manifiesta, entonces, una neurosis emocional - quizás espiritual o existencial - a la vez que el proceso complicado de citas opera en un contexto de ansiedad obsesionante. Tanto frente a sus propias dudas vitales e idealistas como frente a la ansiedad que se revela en el proceso de la cita vemos síntomas de fracaso y de esperanzas malogradas.

¿Cómo explicar este fenómeno? ¿Cómo interpretar este doble ritmo o tensión donde añoranzas por un núcleo inasequible se combinan con un sentido obsesionante de fracaso? En lo que sigue quisiera considerar la poesía machadiana temprana dentro de un contexto que, según yo sepa, nunca se ha planteado. Mientras que un gran número de críticos han destacado las 'influencias' de otros poetas en su obra nadie la ha estudiado dentro del contexto de las 'misprisions' de Harold Bloom ni las seis 'razones revisionarias' elaboradas en *The Anxiety of Influence*.[3] Si en *Los complementarios* y *Juan de Mairena* encontramos a Machado luchando contra sus 'maestros apócrifos fuertes', en la poesía se ve enfrentado a una serie de 'precursores fuertes' ya mencionados, los poetas del siglo anterior y del Siglo de Oro.

'¿Qué buscas, poeta en el ocaso? (*PP*, 482) expresa perfectamente el profundo desasosiego que existe en el fondo de la vida espiritual y artística de Machado. Esta pregunta es bien típica en la época finisecular europea pero la manera de expresar esta problemática y de enfocarla quizás explica el encanto permanente de la poesía anterior a *Campos de Castilla*. Un gran número de estos poemas emplea una serie de imágenes y símbolos que se refieren al topos del viaje o peregrinación. A veces el poeta se llama 'romeo' o 'peregrino'. Este fenómeno tiene que relacionarse con una forma heterodoxa de expresarse espiritualmente en el fin de siglo en España. Es un proceso que no se ha examinado a fondo ni mucho menos comprendido correctamente. Se trata de un estado especial de exaltación artística, cuyo énfasis marcadamente espiritual está arraigado en la condición metafísica de escepticismo y duda finiseculares. Llevaba el nombre de *neomisticismo*.

Uno de los comentaristas más tempranos y acertados fue Urbano González Serrano, krausista, amigo de la Institución Libre, erudito en filosofía, las ciencias y las artes e íntimo del grupo que rodeaba a *Helios*. En 1881, en *Ensayos de crítica y filosofía* notó

> corrientes misteriosas e influencias poderosísimas, de virtualidad innegable, del arte a la religión y viceversa, ... entendiendo que un *ideal estético* puede guiar a un ideal religioso. ... Así, al lado de la paradoja, del dolor y de la desesperación, hállase... un rasgo de energía y virtualidad potentísima, una alta aspiración a algo, que por lo que tiene de vago e indeterminado encanta y seduce y constituye como el bálsamo de consuelo, que restaña heridas aún abiertas. (pp. 93-94)

Dos años más tarde en *Cuestiones contemporáneas* identificó 'una fe invertida' enfrentando el creciente escepticismo. Al final de esta década en un ensayo sobre 'El dolor' pudo averiguar lo heterodoxas de las nuevas tendencias religiosas:

> Avanza la juventud e idealiza el amor hasta llegar al límite de lo místico... el movimiento lógico y expansivo del amor en la *Imitación del Cristo*... [se convierte en] amores... sedientos del ideal. Lo mismo se observa en los poetas. ... La glorificación razonada del sufrimiento es la más sublime apoteosis del amor. Sentir su propia miseria es elevarse por encima de ella; la turbación y el deseo simbolizan la luz y las penumbras de la vida y del amor y la intensidad del amor se mide por la del dolor que produce: 'amar es sufrir, sufrir es amar'.[4]

Alrededor del año 1903 llegó el trágico fin del proceso; González Serrano recordó en *La literatura del día* que el modernismo (la poesía contemporánea) 'huye con honda melancolía de la fe perdida, y emprende la marcha hacia *terra incognita* con la esperanza moral del nuevo Mesianismo, ... con sed insaciable del ideal y llega a ser místico secularizado y heterodoxo o *ateo por bondad*'.[5] 'Oscilan entre su escepticismo y un misticismo cerebral, escape de energías', escribió González Serrano en 1903 (p. 28).

En la misma época, dentro del campo de la poesía, Darío también hablaba del 'sacerdocio del arte' y comparó el papel creador del poeta con el martirio de Cristo destacando a la vez el vaivén angustiado entre un alto Ideal y el abismo del vacío escéptico, tema que ya se había encontrado en Hugo y Baudelaire. Se trata de la busca de una posible salvación mediante el Arte contrastada con un sentido de destrucción inminente. En su ensayo sobre Paul Verlaine en *Los raros* (1896) escribió Darío:

> Era un sublime apasionado, un nervioso, uno de esos divinos semilocos necesarios para el progreso humano, lamentables cristos del arte, que por amor al eterno ideal tienen su calle de la amargura, sus espinas y su cruz. Nació con la adorada llama de la poesía, y ella le alimentaba al propio tiempo que era su martirio. ... Desde muy temprano conoció las asechanzas del lobo racional. ... Su necesidad de análisis, la condición alegraica de su fantasía, hácele producir tristísimos efectos cuando nos arrastra al borde de lo desconocido, la especulación filosófica nubló en él la fe, que debiera poseer como todo poeta verdadero.[6]

Me parece que esta condición y la del *neomisticismo* pueden aplicarse a Antonio Machado. Se nota una constante mezcla de imágenes religiosas con las poéticas, se destacan un profundo escepticismo y una neurosis en cuanto a su sinceridad artística y el poeta se presenta como víctima del vaivén entre un ideal anhelado y un sentido profundo de fracaso. También parece derivar un sentido de placer de su martirio (el 'borracho melancólico', hombre intoxicado de melancolía en lugar de un ebrio sumido en la tristeza por los efectos del alcohol) que, a su vez, aumenta la pasión de su busca de un amor ideal. Y esta condición neomística también se mezcla con el deseo de desplazar y suplantar la literatura mística tradicional en cuyo contexto trabaja.[7] De eso surge otro sentido de inquietud porque reconoce que la 'misprision' que anhela es imposible ya que no puede descartar de su propia poesía las huellas de la tradición anterior. Se encuentra, entonces, en un doble ritmo de inquietud psicológica que también compartieron varios de sus contemporáneos (Darío, Jiménez, Swinburne, Dowson, Laforgue, Reverdy, D'Annunzio, etc.).

La forma fuertemente religiosa del idioma poético de Machado refleja el discurso tradicional teocéntrico de la poesía religiosa española y, muy especialmente, la de San Juan de la Cruz, precursor reconocido. En el momento finisecular de las primeras composiciones machadianas se publicó una serie enorme de artículos y libros sobre varios escritores y poetas religiosos. Los nombres de San Francisco de Asís, Tomás de Kempis, Santa Teresa, Fray Luis de León, entre muchos, se destacaron en las revistas y librerías. Sin embargo se destacó mayormente el nombre de San Juan de la Cruz. En fecha tan temprana como 1881 leyó su *Discurso inaugural* en la Real Academia Española el erudito más célebre de aquel entonces sobre el tema de 'La poesía mística en España'. En este discurso Marcelino Menéndez Pelayo concluyó por decir:

> Ni creamos que morirá la poesía mística, que siempre ha de tener por refugio algunas almas escogidas, aún en este siglo de duda y descreimiento, que nació entre revoluciones apocalípticas, y acaba en su triste senectud, dejándonos en la filosofía un nominalismo grosero, y en el arte de la descripción menuda y fría de los pormenores, descripción por descubrir...[8]

Quizás Machado se vio como una de 'algunas almas escogidas'. El amigo de Machado, Juan Ramón Jiménez, quien leyó y ensalzó este ensayo, al escribir sobre el tema del simbolismo en 1899, rechazó los ataques de los críticos de la Restauración:

> No puedo comprenderlos; simbolistas fueron los más inmortales poetas. ... Nuestro San Juan de la Cruz, de cuya prosa ha dicho Menéndez Pelayo que 'no es de este mundo', fue también eminentemente simbolista...[9]

Me parece que el ambiente cultural era bien propicio para reformular una poesía 'mística' dentro del contexto de la busca de normas eternas, y esto, quizás, explica en parte la inquietud machadiana frente a la poesía mística.

La vía mística por la purgación y la iluminación hasta la unión culminante entre el alma y el esposo está basada sobre el menosprecio del mundo, de las tinieblas amenazadoras y la soledad que aliena. El fin, por contraste, representa una plenitud, una totalidad completa, e anverso del rechazo negador: es la unión positiva del alma y el amado. Sin embargo, a pesar del sueño y la 'bendita ilusión' de que tenía a Dios dentro de su corazón (*PP*, 471), el Machado *neomístico*, por lo general, carecía de fe. Por eso me parece que se debe ligar este fenómeno no sólo con la herencia romántica de duda metafísica sino también con el simbolismo trascendental europeo ya elaborado por Mallarmé entre 1864 y 1865. Mallarmé trataba de crear un mundo ideal por medio de la palabra poética. Pese a haber reconocido que detrás de la realidad que le rodeaba no existía más que un vacío insondable, todavía le quedaba fe en un mundo ideal que quizás yaciera escondido dentro de este vacío. Machado, como Mallarmé, buscaba crear formas alambicadas que fuesen puras esencias mayormente exentas de cualquier eco de la realidad concreta. Conscientemente llenaba su mente previamente vaciada de toda imagen arraigada o fundamentada en lo cotidiano con imágenes de cosas 'ausentes', de nociones 'puras', creadas por su concepción poética. Este acto voluntario se liga con la apariencia de constantes referencias a la religión, a la Biblia y a las afirmaciones de fe expresadas en la poesía de tipo popular. Crean, deliberadamente, la ilusión o efecto de una trayectoria teológica. En realidad, crean una 'mentira vital', un proceso de autoengaño que representa, quizás, la terapéutica más típica del momento finisecular en España, 'el bálsamo de consuelo, que restaña heridas aun abiertas'.[10] En realidad, a pesar de un aparente apego a la religión, a pesar de establecer una trayectoria de creaciones objetivas 'puras' y 'ausentes' siempre le queda, a pesar de sus dudas acerca su papel poético y sus poderes creativos, la idea de un centro o núcleo adonde dirigirse. Se lanza, como su místico precursor, San Juan, en 'una noche oscura' del vacío de su fe desmoronada para encontrar una idea iluminadora. Por fin, como veremos, descubre que la voluntad y la lengua poética son insuficientes para realizar y concretar en arte lo que desea. Por eso la dinámica interior de los versos machadianos se revela como el ritmo mismo de la forma poética, el proceso de formular la palabra 'pura'. Es decir, no es el objetivo - Dios, la amada, ilusiones, el jardín o huerto perdido - lo que le importa en el fondo, sino la energética creación del poema. Se apega a la trayectoria poética misma (la palabra en sí) ya que el contenido (el sentido o objetivo) siempre será (y estará) ausente. Reconoce, como lo hará su contemporáneo, Ferdinand de Saussure, que el sentido no es algo misteriosamente inmanente en un signo sino que es funcional, el resultado de su diferencia respecto a todos los otros signos. La palabra no es un absoluto (*significado*) sino un juego de diferencias (*significante*).

Tenemos así un triple ritmo de inquietud: inquietud frente al precursor 'fuerte' (San Juan); frente al sentido de vacío y ausencia de fe; frente a la incertidumbre sobre el valor de la palabra para conferir significación al mundo. En el poema 'En la desnuda tierra del camino' (*PP*, 444) (llena de ecos de la Biblia), por ejemplo, aunque Machado nota la restauración de la armonía y la unión entre Dios y el hombre en la imagen de la Alianza ('Vuelve la paz al cielo...'), la mayor parte del poema se dedica a socavar este sentido de inminente unión que tendrá lugar en un campo que ofrece ecos del 'huerto ameno deseado' del *Cántico espiritual.*

Deshace el poema precursor para destacar una vía de purgación evocada en palabras de resonancia negativa: 'desnuda tierra', 'espino solitario', 'revuelta umbrosa', 'playa estéril', etc. Esto tiene el efecto de desmoronar la 'realidad' del momento. Dichos elementos también configuran un *paisaje del alma* que simboliza su desasosiego espiritual. Hay que notar que Machado, al mismo tiempo, enfatiza la dificultad de comunicarse con y de expresar lo que busca: 'El salmo verdadero / de tenue voz hoy torna / al corazón, y al labio / la palabra quebrada y temblorosa'. Veremos en adelante lo problemático de la cuestión de una lengua adecuada. Recuerda el poeta el proceso de renovación ('otra vez') y la aparición en 'la bendita soledad' de 'tu sombra'. No obstante la 'misprision' de 'En una noche oscura' y el *Cántico espiritual*, el objeto deseado no tiene forma ni sustancia, carece de identidad. Socava el empuje de las metáforas de la Alianza y el sitio de amores tradicional, es decir, la trayectoria mística que depende de una metafísica de la presencia, el Dios cognoscible. Pese a que la unión pueda ser difícil o postergada, la tradición teológica cree que el Dios ausente es, al fin y al cabo, cognoscible, alcanzable. El 'Otro' de Machado está siempre ausente, evocado en un tiempo pasado, o en sueños o en la memoria; pertenece al mundo de concepciones puras, está exento casi completamente de culquier contacto con la realidad. La fuente del poema (*PP*, 431) (en realidad un alter ego desplazado contra el cual lucha el poeta) - y no olvidar las resonancias teológicas de esta imagen - le pregunta: '¿Te recuerda, hermano, / un sueño lejano mi canto presente?' Sin embargo, queda el poeta incierto y busca saber más del enigmático secreto: 'mas cuéntame, fuente de lengua encantada, / cuéntame mi alegre leyenda olvidada'. En otra 'misprision' de la búsqueda de la Amada de San Juan aquí (y quizás también en el poema siguiente en el símbolo de los limones inalcanzables en la fuente) expresa Machado su propia busca de lo que queda en el 'olvido', en el mundo de Ideas platónico, el reino de *anamnesis* de Fray Luis. 'La alegra leyenda olvidada' repite el sentido de los versos del *Cántico*: 'los ojos deseados, / Que tengo en mis entrañas dibujadas'. La imagen, como la palabra poética que se busca, queda grabada en la memoria aunque no puede reconstruirse en forma absoluta. Persiste la forma - símbolo, metáfora, metonimia (significantes); siempre se escapa la palabra 'pura' (significado). A pesar de la luminosidad de la 'tarde clara' no puede 'ver' en la 'tarde muerta' (el vacío), no puede recobrar el perdido momento de cantos (armonía), mirtos (amor), los frutos maduros (símbolos del Jardín de las Hespérides si no del Jardín de Edén antes de la Caída), no puede vislumbrar a través del 'claro cristal'. La línea recta que sugiere la vía mística positiva (y la trayectoria poética trascendental) se dobla hacia atrás para encerrar al poeta ya que el poema se cierra con la misma estrofa con la cual se abrió.

En 'Cenit' (*PP*, 743) Machado reformula este aspecto en un diálogo semejante. Erige un contraste binario entre el Otro ('tu pensil de *Oriente*') y el poeta y su realidad ('los tristes jardines de *Occidente*'). Busca el poeta una respuesta al 'enigma del presente [que] te inquieta'. Pero la fuente, hablando por su 'salterio' (cosa que también resalta el valor simbólico espiritual) le ofrece un pronunciamiento sibilino: 'Tu destino / será siempre vagar ¡oh peregrino / del laberinto que tu sueño encierra!'; mora en 'un misterio de sombra'; se ve encerrado en el laberinto de sus propios sueños; se ve sumiso en la misma inquietud, la misma sed: 'Dijeron tu pena tus labios que ardían; / la sed que ahora tienen, entonces tenían' (*PP*, 432). Vemos, entonces, la subordinación del objeto deseado a una evocación negativa: negación en forma de purgación de una realidad amena; negación de su propia angustia mediante la objetivación del humor en un *paisaje del alma*; negación de la posibilidad de formular la palabra 'pura', el significado deseado y siempre ausente.

Casi todos los comentaristas han notado la obsesión machadiana con el tiempo. En 'Hacia un ocaso radiante' domina una serie de verbos imperfectos que por su repetición dan una idea de proceso inacabado e inacabable. Lo que busca es la 'hermosa tarde, nota de la lira inmensa / toda desdén y armonía'. La lira (la música celeste del mundo neoplatónico cristiano le atrae ('armonía') a la par que le rechaza ('desdén'). Así, aunque pasa por su vía purgativa (llena de sombras y presagios de muerte) no encuentra la vía iluminativa de la oscuridad que le enamora sino una vuelta al mundo y a la ciudad, símbolo de sus preocupaciones mundanas. Queda solamente un 'lucero diamantino', imagen mística tanto como simbolista del fin inasequible. El poema 'Yo voy soñando caminos' (*PP*, 436) repite explícitamente la imagen del camino. Recrea otro ambiente de oscuridad y silencio - aún de amenaza - que, por el paisaje del alma, se convierte en un sitio de meditación. Pero el camino no parece ir a ninguna parte. Aquí las 'misprisions' de la saeta popular, las 'flechas' de San Juan y de Santa Teresa, y de otros precursores fuertes - Bécquer y Rosalía de Castro - ganan un significado especial.[11] Machado sabía muy bien que en la saeta sevillana y en poemas como 'Llama de amor viva' las flechas o las llamas del deseo (que son los símbolos de la unión o contacto con el objeto anhelado) no se sienten físicamente sino emocional o espiritualmente. La 'misprision' de los dos establece el punto perfectamente por su ambigüedad: que si todavía queda la espina no se puede sentir o si se siente la sensación que queda es la de la flecha quitada (una ausencia) y, así, de un anhelo profundo. En poema tras poema las 'ausencias' simbolistas forman ecos y 'misreadings' de 'la memoria de tanto bien perdido' y 'la vida le es penosa / cuando se halla ajena / de aquella dulce patria tan amena' de la 'Canción de la glosa soberana' y otros poemas similares. Machado, como su precursor místico, enfatiza la separación física y el sentido de pérdida y ausencia combinado con un deseo dolorido. En el poema XLII, quizás una 'misprisión' de *L'Après midi d'un faune* de Mallaramé, renuncia al escenario normal de oscuridad y crepúsculo para situar el encuentro fugaz en la luz deslumbrante del mediodía. Empleando el mito de Artemis, gemela de Apolo, quien hace de la castidad una ley severa y la impuso sobre sus acólitos antes que la historia de las ninfas soñadas de Mallarmé, crea Machado una versión heterodoxa - aún decadente - del viaje místico.[12] En efecto, junto con la 'misreading' de Mallarmé se hallan varias citas de *El cántico espiritual* (y el tema del cazador

24

que hiere) que se mezcla con las flechas de Santa Teresa y la saeta sevillana. Por un momento queda la visión armónica del campo, los animales y la amada cazadora (tanto la mítica Artemis como la Amada del *Cántico*). Pero la caza de la 'fugitiva ilusión' es precismanete eso, una caza ilusoria. El proceso queda incompleto. Ha herido la flecha y se ha concebido la 'idea', no obstante, la consumación de la palabra 'pura' no se ha verificado.[13] A la par que resta una huella de esta herida también queda una 'huella' o 'traza' de intertextualidad del poema sanjuaniano y las tradiciones populares.

En 'Pesadilla', nos presenta Machado una de las expresiones más consumadas de la 'noche oscura del alma'. Se encuentran los mismos elementos que en 'Los sueños malos' (*PP*, 468): una oscuridad creciente, muestras de introspección, aún de soledad y muerte. La soledad del poeta se aumenta por la inaccesibilidad del 'huerto cercano', el jardín perdido, sitio condenado al decaimiento temporal por el efecto simbólico de la hiedra y el ciprés fúnebre. Domina el ruido terrible del agua que 'brota y brota', símbolo del inexorable fluir de todo. Destaca la 'traza' del tema místico donde la fuente (Espíritu divino que da vida eterna) se expresa en su sentido binario. Es decir, el sistema místico funciona por lo que excluye. Demuestra Machado cómo tales oposiciones pueden minarse parcialmente o el proceso por el cual se puede observar que se socavan mutuamente. Como en otras imágenes que emplea Machado su símbolo representa el vacío, la ausencia de valores y principios originarios o un Dios ausente. La fuente vital lo es solamente por excluir este 'otro' o sentido opuesto negativo que se define por la antítesis. Por eso la identidad de ambos se contagia y se pone a riesgo en cualquier esfuerzo que hace cada uno para afirmar sus sendas existencias únicas y autónomas. De ahí la inestabilidad de las imágenes machadianas mediante las 'misreadings' de San Juan; de ahí la veta negativa de su camino espiritual.

En 'Tristezas' (*PP*, 478), ni siquiera puede refugiarse en el mundo de los sueños: 'Hoy buscarás en vano / a tu dolor consuelo. / Lleváronse tus hadas / el lino de tus sueños. / Está la fuente muda, / y está marchito el huerto'. De nuevo las fuerzas negativas y las oposiciones binarias se destacan. Así se retira el poeta hacia un mundo de oscuridad y conexiones perdidas, un mundo de incertidumbre sugerida por la 'misprision' negativa de los símbolos cristianos.

En efecto, el tema de la purgación y la dificultad de la búsqueda mística se mezclan en 'Sobre la tierra amarga' (*PP*, 444). Nunca se puede seguir el sendero laberíntico de direcciones y niveles que cambian, vía cuya dificultad se subraya por una serie de significantes que nunca se resuelven en un significado:

    caminos tiene el sueño

25

laberínticos, sendas tortuosas,
parques en flor y en sombra y en silencio;
criptas hondas, escalas sobre estrellas...

Este mundo de sueños y de retraimiento interior se llena de tinieblas y silencio, vacío de todo menos sombras y presencias que se burlaban de él. Sólo en la distancia inasequible quedan las 'imágenes amigas' quienes le señalan la ruta hacia el jardín escondido más allá de la 'vuelta florida del sendero', eco del verso 'prado de verduras / de flores esmaltado' sanjuaniano. En otros poemas se encuentran las mismas presencias misteriosas. En '¡Tenue rumor' (*PP*, 445) el susurro de la túnica, el *chiton* de la doncella o la diosa griega, le sugiere una Artemis elusiva y esquiva tanto como la amada ausente del poema 'El limonero lánguido' (*PP*, 432), cuya presencia se evoca por la sombra en el muro, el 'aroma de ausencia' y 'algún vagar de túnica ligera'. Y en '¡Tenue rumor', 'blancos fantasmas lares' misteriosos forman un preludio a la unión anhelada y el abrirse para recibir el objeto deseado:

- Abre el balcón. La hora
de una ilusíon se acerca...

En los últimos versos de 'El poeta' (*PP*, 441) se encuentra una idea afín. Evoca Machado 'el jardín encantado de ayer' que le enseña 'el demonio de los sueños'. Aquí el sentido del pasado 'que hermosamente ... fingía la primavera' tiene dentro el binarismo que excluye la afirmación: 'del árbol de otoño estaba el fruto colgado, / mísero fruto podrido, / que el hueco acibarado / guarda el gusano escondido!'. Se desmorona continuamente el valor de la palabra ya que se socava su sentido, cada palabra se deshace y se desliza debajo de otra en una cadena infinita de significantes.

A menudo, parece que el objeto deseado está prácticamente al alcance del peregrino: 'La tarde todavía / dará incienso de oro a tu plegaria' (*PP*, 446). El fin deseado se evoca en términos negativos: 'Mas no es...', 'sino', 'no... ni...'. El poeta se hace un 'romero', pero es un romero opuesto a la tradición, peregrino que busca un lugar santo que no existe y la intercesión de un Dios que está ausente. Desdeña el abrigo de la sombra y el refresco del agua, ya que representan una preparación necesaria para acercar a 'la tierra verde y santa y florecida / de tus sueños'. Otras veces el objeto deseado queda en las tinieblas, distante, inasequible, una imagen incierta y decepcionante que se enfrenta con el poeta solitario y angustiado: 'pesa y duele el corazón'. Al llegar a este objeto, éste se manifiesta como una estrella lejana. En otro poema su amada es a la vez 'esquiva y compañera' (*PP*, 447). No sabe si ella puede exacerbar o consumir sus añoranzas, sentimiento que Machado hábilmente evoca con la imagen del peregrino sediento, motivo que había empleado en otros versos. Sin embargo, las atracciones de la luz, del susurro de la túnica, las caras que se ven en ventanas distantes, la 'ilusión

26

fugitiva' o 'la virgen esquiva', la posibilidad aparente de seguir un camino hacia el fin deseado son núcleos ilusorios e inalcanzables. Al fin le ponen obstáculos el espacio y el tiempo. También se los pone la palabra absoluta, deseada con ansia profunda porque Machado esconde sus inquietudes frente a la ausencia de un centro o núcleo de delineación o definición debajo de las señas confortantes de 'presencia'. El caminante ('romero' o 'peregrino') se encuentra encerrado, encarcelado; pero no se encuentra en una mazmorra de muros fuertes sino en un 'laberinto de espejos', un mundo en el cual cada palabra se quiebra, se desliza de diferencia en diferencia, un mundo inestable de espejismos donde no existe un sentido en que fiarse. Cuando le pregunta al alba (símbolo de una iluminación potencial) si le quedan memorias 'del hada de tu sueño adamantino', ésta le contesta al poeta en términos bien negativos:

> Sólo tienen cristal los sueños míos.
> Yo no conozco el hada de mis sueños;
> ni sé si está mi corazón florido.   (*PP*, 450)

Expresa su conocimiento en términos de una cárcel de cristal, un mundo exento de realidad, un vacío. El provenir incierto sólo le puede traer un hacerse pedazos del 'vaso cristalino' de su cárcel y un momento del *collige virgo rosas*, el encuentro con la perfección y la pureza de un amor sin presencia. Este sentido de encierro aleja al poeta del presente hacia un futuro incierto de unión posible y, más a menudo, hacia la memoria. Allí el deseo por un objeto incognoscible puede sustanciarse en términos de sueños infantiles, lugares rememorados de sol de primavera y verano calientes y una sensualidad implícita. La amada soñada de 'El limonero lánguido' (*PP*, 432), las memorias de 'antiguos delirios de amores' (que se revelan como 'leyendas' antes que 'historias' en 'Fue una clara tarde' (*PP*, 431)) y el 'inventario galante' (*PP*, 455), todos sugieren una dimensión erótica dentro de la busca espiritual.[14]

Pregunta lastimeramente:

> ...¿Dónde están los huertos floridos de rosas?
> ¿Qué dicen las dulces campanas al viento?   (*PP*, 459)

Machado se hace eco del topos clásico del *¿Ubi sunt?* Al cerrar el poema pregunta: '¿Al fin la alegría se acerca a mi casa?' El título del poema - 'Mai piú' - sugiere que nunca habrá un regreso, no podrá haber una vuelta al hogar. Sus añoranzas se hacen desilusión y postración nerviosa frente a la constante ausencia, el vacío de una trayectoria que no va a ninguna parte.

Nunca será posible que el poeta abrace, ni vea ni conozca a la 'virgen', a la 'ilusión', a la amada. Mientras que anuncia el alba la llegada de la esposa / amada, dice el poeta: 'no te verán mis ojos'. En otra 'misprision' de *El cántico espiritual* también aquí se nombra el objeto

27

deseado a través de la voz de los animales y en los elementos naturales; pero, en vez de buscar locamente al amado, Machado no puede más que esperar. Termina el poema en una nota de muerte, pérdida y ausencia, elementos que sugieren quizás un episodio autobiográfico relacionado al objeto deseado ausente. El poeta solamente puede conocer parcialmente a la amada, nunca puede consumarse en la plenitud de la unión; es decir que hace un símbolo para expresar su dilema frente a la palabra inasequible y el sentido infinitamente postergado. Siente dolorosamente la frustración de su apego y, en 'El rojo sol de un sueño' (*PP*, 484), reconoce que la tierra prometida y la consumación deseada nunca serán suyas. Entra en el mundo de la iluminación:

> Luz en sueños. ¿No tiemblas, andante peregrino?
> Pasado el llano verde, en la florida loma,
> acaso está el cercano final de tu camino.

El peregrino, como la amada en *El cántico espiritual*, pasa por el 'campo recién florido y verde' de los salmos pero no lo 'conoce': '¡quién pudiera / soñar aún largo tiempo en esas pequeñitas / corolas azuladas que manchan la pradera...!' No ha entrado 'en el ameno huerto deseado' del *Cántico*. No puede quedarse en la contemplación del mundo que le rodea, tiene que buscar más allá. Pero, como dice el título - 'Presentimiento' -, la experiencia no es nada más que eso. La consumación anhelada se le niega perpetuamente, como le dice la voz en 'Cenit' que le condena al 'laberinto que tu sueño encierra!' (*PP*, 743). La metáfora del 'laberinto' expresa la dificultad de la vía mística pero también funciona como un *mise en abyme* de significantes dentro de significantes, una cadena infinita de diferencias metonímicas que nunca se anclarán en el objeto deseado, el centro trascendental.

Y, en efecto, una visión directa del objeto deseado le destruiría, como predijo Darío en su ensayo sobre Verlaine y San Juan en sus cánticos. En 'El poeta' (*PP*, 441) Machado recuerda (en tiempo imperfecto):

> Y viendo como lucían
> miles de blancas estrellas,
> pensaba que todas ellas
> en su corazón ardían
> ¡Noche de amor!

No obstante, la 'pura llama' se ve cargada de peligros:

> Y otra noche
> sintió la mala tristeza
> que enturbia la pura llama,
> y el corazón que bosteza,
> y el histrión que declama.

> Y dijo: las galerías
> del alma que espera están
> desiertas, mudas, vacías:
> las blancas sombras se van.

Cuando se retira el velo se le revela la amenaza del tiempo y la muerte tanto como sus propias dudas en lo que a su papel poético se refiere, su propia insinceridad y su desasosiego. Recuerda al 'demonio de mi sueño' y 'el ángel más hermoso' (*PP*, 474). Aquí le muestra al peregrino una luz brillante que le trae miedo y terror. En la poesía compañera (*PP*, 474) - raramente - 'la voz querida' le viene sin ser invitada y le conduce hacia su centro. Así huye de la luz, la mirada escudriñadora del 'demonio' y el martirio-consuelo de su visión para abrazar al 'otro' en las tinieblas o en una forma de muerte incipiente. En 'Campo' (*PP*, 482) el paisaje del alma evoca un viaje hacia la oscuridad de la noche, hacia las ascuas de la luz misma, hacia la propia muerte de la vida ('una hoja marchita y negra en cada rama') donde le espera 'los álamos de oro, / lejos, la sombra del amor'. En otra 'misprision', esta vez del mito de los Bosques Dorados de Helicón donde se encuentran las Musas y los frutos dorados de Apolo, hace Machado que la noche esconda la promesa de una nueva luz que, a su vez, irá a amenazar a la 'noche oscura del alma', la noche enamorada. La vía, ahora más difícil, ahora laberíntica, ahora guiándole hacia arriba o abajo, le conduce por una cadena de imágenes: caminos que se cruzan, sendas tortuosas, criptas hondas, escalas sobre estrellas, etc. Al fin la vía se hace un círculo sin término, una cárcel espacial y temporal. Para romper el círculo tiene que dejar su búsqueda, cesar de desear, de 'conocer' en el sentido racional. Por haber preguntado, como indica '¡Oh, dime, noche amiga' (*PP*, 451), se encuentra encarcelado en sus propias dudas acerca de su peregrinación, su sinceridad, aún el fundamento de su búsqueda. Y en otra 'misprision' de San Juan crea un coloquio entre el Amado y la Amada:

> ¡dime, si sabes, vieja amada, dime
> si son mías las lágrimas que vierto!
> Me respondió la noche:
> Yo nunca supe, amado,
> si eras tú ese fantasma de tu sueño,
> ni averigüé si era su voz la tuya,
> o era la voz de un histrión grotesco.

El poeta se representa a sí mismo como confuso, extraviado espiritualmente. No sabe si el objeto deseado es un 'Otro' o si es una representación de sus propios deseos. Cuando dice 'creo', como Unamuno, no sabe si 'cree' or 'crea'. Es decir, no sabe si la amada existe fuera de su propio ser de poeta o si forma parte de su propio gesto histriónico. A pesar de todas las tentativas para prepararse espiritualmente todavía le queda la necesidad de reconocer que el centro es incognoscible cuando no inalcanzable y, quizás, que su poesía, 'el salmo verdadero', no puede referirse a ninguna cosa. Por eso el 'significado' no puede nombrarse; la única cosa que puede ofrecer el poeta es una cadena de 'significantes' que se pliega sobre sí misma en un *mise en abyme* de auto-referencialidad. La lengua poética se transforma en un laberinto o una serie de espejos dentro de espejos de autocontemplación y auto-memoria que nunca pueden nombrar al 'Otro'. La 'interior bodega' de San Juan se convierte en otra metáfora:

> escucho su hondo rezo,
> humilde y solitario,
> ese que llamas salmo verdadero,
> pero en las hondas bóvedas del alma
> no sé si el llanto es una voz o un eco.

> Para escuchar tu queja de tus labios
> ya te busqué en tu sueño,
> y allí te vi vagando en un borroso
> laberinto de espejos.

En última instancia, como sugieren varios poemas importantes, reconoce que lo innombrable nunca puede buscarse, lo innombrable nunca puede nombrarse. Si el objeto deseado ha de verse de alguna forma tiene que ser como una 'ausencia', mediante la invisibilidad del 'Otro'. En el poema clave, 'Introducción' (*PP*, 472), la 'verdad divina', como la flor mallarméana (y quizás se encuentra aquí otra 'misprision' de otro precursor fuerte), es una flor *in posse* antes que *in esse*, 'una flor que *quiere* echar su aroma al viento'.[15] El aroma está siempre y por toda la eternidad en el momento de echarse al viento; es posible que nunca lo haga. No se puede ver el objeto (como no se puede ver 'el aroma'); no obstante, sabe el poeta que está a su lado aunque infinitamente postergado:

> El alma del poeta
> se orienta hacia el misterio.
> Sólo el poeta puede
> mirar lo que está lejos
> dentro del alma, en turbio
> y mago sol envuelto.

En el poema apropiadamente titulado 'Renacimiento' (*PP*, 486) reafirma Machado la naturaleza del proceso del no saber con una serie de adjetivos negativos:

> En nuestras almas todo
> por misteriosa mano se gobierna.
> Incomprensibles, mudas,
> nada sabemos de las almas nuestras.

Como en el *Cántico espiritual*, la presencia del objeto deseado está en todas partes y, a la vez, en ninguna parte, escondida dentro de los elementos naturales:

> Las más hondas palabras
> del sabio nos enseñan,
> lo que el silbar del viento cuando sopla,
> o el sonar de las aguas cuando ruedan.

Y cuando se cierra 'Introducción' en un tipo de unión redentora de sangre vertida ('sentimos una ola / de sangre, en nuestro pecho, que pasa...') en 'Renacimiento' se hace un eco complicado donde combina Machado una serie de 'misprisions': mezcla las metáforas esenciales de la 'música olvidada' de Fray Luis, la sangre redentora de los Evangelios y la 'música callada' y la lengua alusiva y negadora de San Juan de la Cruz:

> Tal vez la mano, en sueños,
> del sembrador de estrellas,
> hizo sonar la música olvidada
> como una nota de la lira inmensa,
> y la ola humilde a nuestros labios vino
> de unas pocas palabras verdaderas.

No es una coincidencia que el verbo con que termina el segundo verso en la segunda estrofa se haga eco del 'vino' simbólico de la Eucaristía ya que, como los místicos, Machado busca una manera adecuada de expresar sus profundos anhelos espirituales. Simbólicamente 'bebe' la 'palabra' que encarna el Espíritu divino, el Otro.

Al encenderse la luz y oscurecerse las sombras, al cesar su curso el agua y al quedar el mundo en el umbral de la muerte misma, se encuentra al amor alado y desnudo. Mazclando el mito de Cupido y el motivo del amor divino en '¿Mi corazón se ha dormido?' (*PP*, 471), Machado los emplea dentro del contexto de un paisaje del alma simbolista. En el plano simbólico - el paisaje del alma del no expresarse, de sentido ausente - encontramos un humor de tranquilidad, el sentimiento de vacío, de una pasividad total, la suspensión de todos los sentidos normales de la vida poética donde la imaginación parece que se ha secado:

> ¿Mi corazón se ha dormido?
> Colmenares de mis sueños
> ¿ya no labráis? ¿Está seca
> la noria de mi pensamiento,
> los cangilones vacíos,
> girando de sombra llenos?[16]

Frente a este sentido de agotamiento y vacío, de pérdida de su potencia creadora (aquí el tema de la búsqueda espiritual se enlaza estrechamente con la problemática estética y por eso nos encontramos en la dimensión *neomística* finisecular) erige Machado una experiencia

31

personal, un humor especial definido por negativos, una extraña forma sobrenatural de ver, una 'misprision' de la 'soledad sonora' de San Juan:

> No, mi corazón no duerme.
> Está despierto, despierto.
> Ni duerme ni sueña, mira,
> los claros ojos abiertos,
> señas lejanas y escucha
> a orillas del gran silencio.

Espera escuchar en este 'silencio' la 'música callada' de los místicos. 'Elegía de un madrigal' (*PP*, 463) reconoce el fracaso de sus 'rimas' en lo que al captar sus memorias ('ondas', 'luz de los cabellos') se refiere. 'La letra mata', dice; busca crear formas que son puras esencias, exenta de cualquier eco de la realidad concreta. Por eso evoca 'aromas', imagen de la rosa 'ausente', una noción pura creada en su concepción poética. Y, en una 'misprision' de la 'llama de amor viva' de San Juan describe la unión momentánea:

> Y un día - como tantos - al aspirar un día
> aromas de una rosa que en el rosal se abría,
> brotó como una llama de luz en los cabellos
> que él en sus madrigales llamaba rubias olas,
> brotó, porque un aroma igual tuvieron ellos...

La afirmación más clara de la consumación, y - cosa que otros discutirán - el poema más religioso entre todos es 'Anoche cuando dormía' (*PP*, 471). Lázaro Carreter ha ligado las imágenes de 'fuente', 'abeja' y 'sol' con las tres virtudes teológicas: fe, esperanza y amor.[17] No obstante, esta interpretación gana más valor en el presente contexto del neomisticismo finisecular. Y esta afirmación viene al caso cuando se reconoce que San Juan, Santa Teresa y la poesía popular religiosa se rinden en este poema a una 'misprision', 'misreading', para expresar la fusión de la búsqueda espiritual de un Dios que no existe con un ideal estético que consuela. En este poema vemos la culminación de esta búsqueda, la negación del objeto deseado. Machado pasa de una metafísica de presencia a una metafísica de ausencia. Se niega o se esconde cada elemento: 'acequia escondida, en donde nunca bebí'; enfatiza el sentido de profundidad interior por el repetido 'dentro', haciendo un *mise en abyme* infinito; la luz, como en 'La noche oscura' y 'Llama de amor viva' ciega y hiere al dar alegría y calor. Y como San Juan, el precursor fuerte, expresa Machado la unión directa y sencillamente:

> Anoche cuando dormía
> soñé, ¡bendita ilusión!,
> que era Dios lo que tenía
> dentro de mi corazón.

Pero la experiencia ocurre dentro de sus sueños y se puede negar porque el poeta no puede averiguar 'si era la voz la tuya, / o era la voz de un histrión grotesco'. Es decir, duda, desde su condición de inquietud profunda, si la palabra que crea se arraiga en un 'Otro' fuera de sí mismo; duda, preocupado, en cuanto a la autenticidad de sus versos, si son 'palabras verdaderas' o si, por el contrario, representan un balbuceo de un poseído, el 'histrión grotesco'.[18] Para salir del doble dilema Machado se enfrenta con el contexto de su deseo, su fe vacilante y sus dudas acerca de la posibilidad de imaginar un Otro. La combinación de sus 'misreadings' de San Juan, su comprensión total de las estéticas del simbolismo y el impacto de las filosofías nietzscheanas del devenir e infinito retorno crean una situación lingüística única. Si el contexto de deseo ha sido siempre la unión con una otredad total, en este caso, reconociendo la presumida ausencia del Otro, se hace su deseo, expresado mediante la palabra poética, una señal sin sentido, vacía. Su deseo se ve negado, borrado. El significado siempre se transforma en un significante que se revela ausente y vice versa. El sentido de una palabra se divide, se difiere, el significado se ausenta del significante. El sentido nunca puede estar completamente 'presente' en una palabra porque siempre se ve esparcido por la cadena de significados a la vez presente y ausente. Cada palabra en la cadena del sentido lleva huellas de todas las otras y también huellas de la poesía mística de los precursores. Al reproducirse en nuevos contextos el significado se ve dividido con respecto a su identidad y así está siempre ausente de sí mismo. Ya que la poesía mística tradicional se fundamenta en un Dios presente, un Dios por descubrir, se ha acostumbrado a erigir baluartes ideológicas o 'metafísicas'. No obstante una metafísica de 'presencia', siempre contiene dentro de su discurso, aunque marginado, un sentido antitético. La poesía de Machado obra sobre la tradición anterior no sólo en una 'misprision' sino también para apoderarse de varias oposiciones binarias inherentes. Lo consigue, especialmente, como hemos visto, explotando las posibilidades del juego entre 'propio ser' y 'Otro', donde cada elemento socava y rinde vacío o impotente al otro. El mismo fenómeno se encuentra operando entre un Dios presente y el ausente que tiene el efecto de minar cualquier forma de teleología cuando no de teología. Por esto la poesía machadiana nos demuestra el profundo escepticismo del autor y de su momento histórico en lo que a su confianza en el concepto de escribir (o crear artísticamente) se refiere.

Su 'escritura' forma un reto a la idea misma de una teleología (religiosa o artística) o de una estructura. Una teleología o estructura siempre supone un centro, un núcleo o punto fijo, un fundamento básico, una jerarquía de sentidos. La poesía machadiana pone en tela de juicio no sólo la ideología de una metafísica de presencia sino también cualquier creencia en la posibilidad de crear, mediante el Arte, un 'Otro', un Ideal, una 'religión'. El juego infinito de sentidos que carecen de una significación pura o fija se enfrenta con cualquier posibilidad de crear un sistema lingüístico en el cual se arraiga una teleología (ya religiosa ya artística). Es decir, la poesía de Machado nos revela el proceso inconsciente de su inquietud ya que a cada punto sentimos la imposibilidad de anclarse, mediante la palabra artística, en una estructura o una metafísica. Al mismo tiempo vemos al Machado consciente rechazando la posibilidad de hacerse auténtico mediante la creación de un 'Otro', dudando de la sinceridad de cada palabra que escribe. Y mediante las 'misreadings' de sus precursores fuertes le vemos también dudando de su propia potencia artística.

Por fin, sólo le queda la trayectoria poética misma (símbolo de la teología ausente). Esta trayectoria se convierte en una cadena de metáforas vacías que, a su vez, forma un encadenamiento absoluto de significantes lingüísticos. Por eso, son las palabras antes que el sentido de los versos machadianos las que son la llave poética del poeta simbolista sevillano. Por eso, y no por razones adventicias, pertenece Machado a la veta posrromántica del simbolismo decimonónico y de la tradición más pura del simbolismo de Mallarmé.[19]

La vía negativa del neomisticismo que emprende Machado, como reconoció González Serrano, es un camino heterodoxo. Lo que arriesga es su propia aniquilación espiritual. Una lengua poética de 'presencia' se fundamenta en la presencia de un 'Otro'. Como comenta Eagleton en su célebre discusión del elemento 'logocéntrico' en la filosofía de Occidente, este sistema se ha visto

> comprometido con la creencia en una 'palabra' última, presencia, esencia, verdad o realidad que hará las veces de fundamento de todo nuestro pensamiento. Ha añorado el signo que dará sentido a todos los otros - el 'significante trascendental' - y punto de partida incuestionable hacia el cual se ven dirigidos todos nuestros signos (el 'significado trascendental'). Un gran número de candidatos para este papel - Dios, la Idea, el Espíritu del Mundo, el Propio Ser, sustancia, materia y demás cosas - se han lanzado a la palestra de vez en vez. Dado que cada uno de estos conceptos espera *fundar* nuestro sistema entero de pensamiento y lengua, ha de hallarse fuera de este sistema, no manchado por su juego de diferencias lingüísticas. No puede implicarse dentro de las mismas lenguas que trata de ordenar y anclar: de alguna manera debe ser anterior a estos discursos, debe haber existido antes que ellos. Debe ser un sentido, pero no como cualquier sentido que no es más que un juego de diferencias. Antes debe figurar como el sentido de los sentidos, el eje o fulcro de un sistema entero de pensamiento, el signo alrededor del cual giran los otros y que reflejan obedientemente todos los otros'.[20]

Machado, también, busca un centro o núcleo en el cual erigir una fe. Para consolarse su desasosiego metafísico, su incertidumbre en lo que a sus poderes creativos se refiere y su duda frente al valor de la palabra poética erige primero una metafísica de 'presencia', la creencia de que puede expresar la Idea absoluta que se encuentra más allá de la realidad por medio de la palabra poética. Luego, descubre que, frente al constante vacío que vislumbra, ha de crear no un 'Ser' sino la 'Ausencia', no la Unidad sino la diseminación, diferencia. Esto, a su vez, le conduce a desplazar su trayectoria desde la búsqueda de un 'significado trascendente' a la trayectoria del propio ritmo de escribir, de crear palabras, la nueva Ley de la palabra de un poeta enteramente simbolista. Quizás Machado reconoció, filósofo sutil como era, que 'lo espiritual no se presenta como sustancia sostenible pero, antes, mediante su ausencia; Dios se hace real, no por la encarnación, sino por la Ley [la Sagrada Escritura]'.[21]

Antonio Machado, como poeta finisecular que escribió dentro del contexto de la religión del Arte, supo encarnar y hacer real su Dios mediante la ley diferencial de la Poesía. Como uno de los poetas simbolistas españoles más destacados fue también el Sumo Sacerdote de la religión de Ausencia. El viaje hacia la realización de este fin fue condicionado por su inquietud frente al ausente pero siempre presente San Juan de la Cruz.

NOTAS

1 G. Ribbans, 'Prólogo' a *Soledades, galerías y otros poemas* (Barcelona: Editorial Labor, 1975), pág. 22.

2 En la primera versión de 'El limonero lánguido' (*PP*, 432) publicado en *Helios*, I, I, vii, julio de 1903, el poema empezaba con dos versos iniciales, luego suprimidos: 'El suelo de piedra y musgo; en las paredes / blancas agarra desgreñada higuera...'.

3 'This short book offers a theory of poetry by way of poetic influence, or the story of intra-poetic relationships. [...] Poetic history, in this book's argument, is held to be indistinguishable from poetic influence, since strong poets make that history by misreading one another, so as to clear imaginative space for themselves. My concern is only with strong poets, major figres with a persistence to wrestle with their strong precursors, even to the death. Weaker talents idealise; figures of capable imagination appropriate for themselves. [...] Poetic influence, or as I shall more frequently term it, poetic misprision, is necessarily the study of the life-cycle of the poet-as-poet', H. Bloom, *The Anxiety of Influence* (Oxford: Oxford University Press, 1975), págs. 5, 7 y 8. También formula seis modos o 'revisionary ratios' dentro de los cuales puede operar la influencia, incluso el proceso de 'misreading' ('misleer').

4 U. González Serrano, *En pro y en contra (Críticas)* (Madrid: s.f.), págs. 224-25.

5 U. González Serrano, 'El Satanismo y el modernismo en el arte', *La literatura del día (1900 a 1903)* (Barcelona: Henrich, 1903), págs. 33-34.

6 Rubén Darío, *Obras completas* (Madrid: Afrodisio Aguado, 1950), II, 267-69.

7 Se puede relacionar este proceso de redescubrimiento de la literatura del pasado con la influencia sobre el pensamiento de varios escritores finiseculares analizada por H. Ramsden en *The 1898 Movement in Spain* (Manchester: University Press, 1974).

8 M. Menéndez y Pelayo, 'La poesía mística en España', *Estudios de crítica histórica y literaria* (Santander: Aldus, 1941), II, 109.

9 Juan Ramón Jiménez, *Libros de prosa* (Madrid: Aguilar, 1969), págs. 211-12. Las palabras que cita se publicaron en *Ensayos de crítica filosófica* (Madrid, 1892), II, 97.

10   Como expresiones típicas de este fenómeno cito dos ejemplos: '"La página blanca" es como un sueño cuyas visiones simbolizaran las bregas, las angustias, las penalidades del existir, la fatalidad genial, las esperanzas y los desengaños, y el irremisible epílogo de la sombra eterna, del desconocido más allá. ¡Ay! Nada ha amargado más las horas de meditación de mi vida que la certeza tenebrosa del fin. ¡Y cuántas veces me he refugiado en algún paraíso articial, poseído del horror fatídico de la muerte!'. Rubén Darío , *Historia de mis libros (1909)*, en *Obras completas* , I, págs. 210-11. En *Del sentimiento trágico de la vida (1913)*, Unamuno hablaba del hombre quien 'adopta distintas actitudes y busca por modos consolarse... Y han hecho del arte una religión y un remedio para el mal metafísico', *Obras completas* (Madrid: Afrodisio Aguado, 1958), XVI, págs. 178-79.

11   Rafael Ferreres, 'La flecha alegórica con que hiere el Amor' en *Los límites del modernismo* (Madrid: Taurus, 1964), págs. 123-31.

12   Artemis era la hermana gemela de Apolo y diosa de la luz lunar. Se la representa armada con un arco, flechas y un carcaj hechos de oro brillante y vestida de una túnica dórica color de azafrán con orlas escarlatas y sandalias. En la tradición se dedicó a la caza en los bosques umbrosos seguida por sus ninfas devotas. Les impuso la castidad y solía matar cruelmente a los hombres que se atrevían a acercarse a curiosear dentro de su territorio. Llevaba como emblema un arco en forma de la luna nueva, un ciervo y una abeja. Machado hizo uso de varios mitos claves, incluso éste, como sugerí en 'Symbolist Solipsism: Musing on Mirrors and Myths', *Language and Literature - Theory and Practice: A Tribute to Walter Grauberg*, ed. C.S. Butler, R.A. Cardwell and J. Channel (Nottingham: University Monographs in the Humanities, núm. VI, 1989), págs. 83-99.

13   Comparar: 'y haciendo por que mueras / las flechas que recibes / de lo que del Amado en ti concibes?' del *Cántico*.

14   Ver, por ejemplo, el sentido erótico que esconden estos versos: 'juncos tiernos, / lánguidos y amarillos' (*PP*, 449) de evidente índole decadente.

15   Me refiero a la célebre cita de Mallarmé: 'Je dis: une fleur! et, hors de l'oubli où ma voix relègue aucun contour, en tant que quelque chose d'autre que les calices sus, musicalement se lève, idée même et suave, l'absente de tous bouquets', *Oeuvres completes* (París: Pléiade, 1945), pág. 857.

16.   Ver también 'El sol es un globo de fuego' (*PP*, 445) donde muere la luz, la paloma (símbolo del Espíritu Santo) vuelve al ciprés (el árbol de la muerte). Los mirtos (simbolizando la presencia de Venus y el Amor) se asocian con el tiempo y el decaimiento en contraste con el único símbolo de vida en este paisaje espiritual simbolista que es la fuente que corre continuamente. Los ecos de Fray Luis y San Juan se destacan.

17   F. Lázaro Carreter, 'Glosa a un poema de Antonio Machado', *Insula*, 119 (noviembre de 1955), pág. 11.

18   Ver mi 'Mirrors and Myths: Antonio Machado and the Search for Self' de próxima aparición en *Romance Studies*.

19   Ver, por ejemplo, los argumentos de G.W. Ribbans en 'Antonio Machado's Attitude to Symbolism', en *Waiting for Pegasus. Studies in the Presence of Symbolism and Decadence in Hispanic Letters*, ed. R. Grass y W.R. Risley (Macomb, Illinois: Western Illinois University, 1979), págs. 39-56, con los cuales no estoy completamente de acuerdo.

20   T. Eagleton, *Literary Theory. An Introduction* (Oxford: Basil Blackwell, 1983), pág. 131.

21   Citado por Emmanuel Lévinas de Susan Handelman en 'Jacques Derrida and the Heretic Hermeneutic', en *Displacement: Derrida and After*, ed. Mark Krupnick (Bloomington: Indiana University Press , 1988), pág. 115.

Editing *Campos de Castilla*

GEOFFREY RIBBANS

Brown University

The average reader of Machado does not, I imagine, find any difficulty in identifying the book we call *Campos de Castilla*. It constitutes a recognizable section of *Poesías completas* and has been published separately on several occasions since the poet's death. Yet, as we know, the book raises a number of problems. There is only one independent publication entitled *Campos de Castilla* issued during the poet's lifetime - the edition of 1912, and this contains only a part - in fact, only about half - of the poems we think of as essential to the collection. Such insecurity about the exact content of Machado's collections of poetry is not new. *Soledades* (1903) is not just a first version of *Soledades. Galerías. Otros poemas* (1907), as Machado stated, and the so-called second edition of SGOP (1919) has major differences from the first; Macrí, with some justification, calls it an anthology of *Poesías completas*.[1]

What is loosely referred to as 'the second edition' of *Campos de Castilla* is not an independent publication, but merely a section of *Poesías completas*. Even more curious is the fact that when this second stage took shape, in the first edition of *Poesías completas*, published by Renacimiento, in 1917, the very title of the section was omitted. Was this omission deliberate or inadvertent, 'una strana distrazione', as Macrí calls it (77)? I shall leave discussion of this question for a moment.

There are doubts, too, about its content. Only a certain number of the poems refer directly to the Castilian landscape indicated in the title; sections like 'Elogios', and titles like 'Proverbios y cantares' - constant since well before the publication of the book - or the related 'Parábolas' have no direct connection with the central theme, and in the second stage poems with a different geographical centre - Baeza, and Andalusia in general - or wider national concerns, are added. Even 'Retrato', which introduces the collection, has little to do with the Castilian landscape.

Finally, there is uncertainty as to which poems make up the collection. Some to-ing and fro-ing of poems between this and other collections occurs; for example, 'Eran ayer mis dolores' (*PP*, 485) included within the SGOP section of PC, is found among the 'Proverbios y cantares' of *Campos de Castilla*. The 'Elogios' also move about from one collection to another

38

and there is some doubt as to whether they belong as of right to *Campos de Castilla* or are there simply for convenience.

Does all this justify our casting doubt on the independent existence of the collection after 1912, as a recent critic, Carlos Moreno Hernández, has suggested?

> La simple constatación de estos datos, soslayados o ignorados normalmente por la crítica, no sólo indica que no existe un libro *Campos de Castilla* ampliado en 1917, sino que hace sospechar que Machado, por estas fechas, estaba en clara vacilación respecto a su 'obra esbozada en *Campos de Castilla*' que tenía la pretensión de continuar unos años antes ... y sobre el destino que debía dar a los poemas escritos en su mayor parte entre 1907 y 1917, junto a algunos anteriores.[2]

I would certainly not go so far, and am much more inclined to attribute the absence of title in 1917 to a non untypical bit of Machadian forgetfulness. His hatred of proof reading is well attested, and could easily account for this omission. I personally cannot see how Machado could possibly make a deliberate decision to allow these very important, personal poems, especially the so-called 'ciclo de Leonor', to appear with a distinctive title, hidden beneath an insipid heading from the previous collection, 'Varia'.

Moreover, the uncertainties I am speaking of are apt to occur on the margins of the essential core of the collection and are to some extent to be explained by the special and traumatic experience Machado suffered in the loss of his wife, an experience insolubly tied up with the collection itself.

What problems does all this pose for an editor with any claims to prepare a critical or, at all events, critically useful edition? I put it that way, because there is no question of competing with Oreste Macrí's superb edition, which has, according to an advertisement in *Insula*, just made a most welcome appearance in a Spanish edition by the Fundación Antonio Machado and el Ministerio de Cultura.

I had hoped to have copies available of my new edition in Cátedra, but you will have to make do with my explanations and comments. The choice of a reliable text was not difficult, since the starting point must be *Poesías completas*, the last edition (the fourth, 1936) published in his lifetime; the section bearing the title 'Campos de Castilla' also has a useful chronological delimitation: '1907-1917', which I have borne in mind by including in an appendix any other poem known to have been written between these dates. I have also provided some necessary ancillary material to elucidate the text.

More difficult was to establish as accurately as possible, from all the sources available, the date of publication of all the poems of the collection, utilizing not only the two 'editions' in book form, but the many poems published in reviews, and including, at the same time, all the rearrangement of material and variants introduced in the various stages of publication. Macrí's edition is invaluable here, but I have been able to add a little additional data. Finally, I have set out to assess and interpret this varied material, both regarding its internal implications within the corpus of Machado's work and in relation to the poet's life.

Obviously, in the time at my disposal, I can't go into all the implications of these criteria now. I propose therefore to limit myself to considering what a scrupulous chronology and a close attention to variants can tell us about the evolution of the poet and to chance my arm with a few suggestions.

On the accompanying sheets I have listed, as far as we know them, the date of first publication - or of composition, if we have reasonably strong evidence on this point - of the poems of *Campos de Castilla*. I have divided them into four sections: the poems published before the 1912 edition; those first published in that edition; those which appeared between 1912 and 1917; and finally, those poems for which we have no earlier publication date than *Poesías completas* of 1917.

Let me now comment on some aspects of this listing. First, in the pre-*Campos de Castilla* publications, it is worth noting that four 'elogios' of earlier date (CXLVI, CXLVII, CLI, CLII) are included. These are dedicated, significantly, to the four writers Machado very possibly most admired and who are, from whatever viewpoint one adopts, the most eminent writers of their time: Valle-Inclán, Rubén Darío, Unamuno and Juan Ramón Jiménez. These are thus accorded an honoured place in a growing pantheon of modern figures worthy of praise.

Second, the significant date of 'Retrato', which appeared in *El Liberal* on 1 February 1908, less than five months after Antonio took up residence in Soria.[3] In my view, it is thus the poem which best exemplifies his state of mind as he takes up his new career, even though it shows as yet no sign of response to his new environment. His famous rejection of the artificial and frivolous values of the literary Bohemia takes on a different aspect in the light of his very recent decision to take a job. In so doing, he is not only asserting his own personality but also separating himself by implication from those who devote themselves to nothing but literature. Hence his proud declaration that he pays his own way, offering his poetry for free:

Y al cabo, nada os debo: debéisme cuanto he escrito.

A mi trabajo acudo, con mi dinero pago
el traje que me cubre y la mansión que habito,
el pan que me alimenta y el lecho en donde yago.   (*PP*, 492)

A third feature is the striking absence of any substantial number of poems published between 1907 and 1912. In the autumn of 1907, when he already resided in Soria, the last poems (among them some of the most introspective)[4] included in *SGOP* appeared in reviews, followed in November by the collection itself. From then on, until the end of 1908 - more than a year - the only poem we know to have been published is 'Retrato'. Then comes the not very typical poem 'Fantasía iconográfica' (December 1908; 11; CVII) and the first 'Proverbios y cantares', published in February 1909. By May 1909 we have 'Amanecer de otoño' (13; CIX) and 'Pascua de Resurrección' (16; CXII) and more 'Proverbios y cantares'. 'Hoy he visto una monjita', part of 'En tren' (14; CX), dates from September. In these verses, and perhaps in those of 'Pascua de Resurrección', we catch a glimpse - no more than a glimpse - of his attraction for Leonor, as he broaches the subject of young girls approaching marriage ('madrecitas en flor') and the preference of his girl 'por un barbero lampiño'.

At the time of his marriage, then, in July 1909, Machado is not yet the poet of the Sorian countryside. It is remarkable that there was no rapid follow-up of 'Orillas del Duero' (XI), included at the last minute in *SGOP* as a result of a fleeting visit to Soria in May 1907. We have to wait until February 1910 for the first Castilian descriptive and interpretative poem, 'A orillas del Duero' (2; XCVIII), and until December for another poem on the same theme: 'Por tierras de España' (3; XCIX). As far as we know, he published no new poem in 1911. An extraordinarily limited crop of eight poems published in four years, a period moreover when his new life, both professional and personal, might have been expected to give rise to increased poetic activity. No doubt there were other poems, and he was reserving their first publication for his forthcoming and much delayed new volume; Carlos Beceiro may well be right in believing that the first poems of the collection - the most critical ones - were composed in 1908 or 1909,[5] but his public silence during this time - commented on, for example, by Villaespesa - is nonetheless strange.[6]

It is significant that the first of the Castilian poems in the collection, as far as we know, should be *A orillas del Duero*, which, as Arthur Terry has demonstrated so effectively, established a mood within the framework of his personal exertions as he walks and climbs just outside Soria.[7] Only when this 'sense of a landscape' - to use Terry's term - has been captured does the poet seek to give his famous interpretation of the course of the Castilian past and its relationship with the present. We may or may not accept this interpretation - I share Terry's view that these passages are 'less subtle and well-written than the rest of the poem'

(26) - but it is an essential part of the poem and of Machado's complex attitude towards the Castilian landscape.

When we turn to *Campos de Castilla* (1912), we have a slim volume, which, if we count all the 29 'Proverbios y cantares' under one title, contains only 17 poems (46 if we consider each separately); some of the best-known Castilian poems such as 'Orillas del Duero' and 'El Dios ibero' are not included. In this handful of poems, *La tierra de Alvargonzález* (with 712 lines) occupies a disproportionate space: almost half. The other extensive poem, *Campos de Soria* (with 144 lines), takes up about 10% of the collection.

Another matter of interest is its tardy publication. Pérez Ferrero assures us that the manuscript was ready and in the hands of the printing house Renacimiento before Antonio and Leonor left for Paris at the beginning of 1911, just after Epiphany or *Reyes*.[8] On his return Machado complains twice, in letters to Juan Ramón, about how long it is taking to publish.[9] Though there is no reason not to accept Pérez Ferrero's statement, what is in doubt is the exact content of the original text. It has been known for a long time (Pérez Ferrero, 133) that *La tierra de Alvargonzález* was added later. We now know, thanks to Carlos Beceiro, that *Campos de Soria* appeared in an incomplete form, significantly different from the final version, in March 1907, only a couple of months before the book itself. This obviously raises the serious doubt as to whether the final version of *Campos de Soria* was in the original manuscript or even whether the poem was included at all.[10] The manuscript submitted in 1910 was certainly much slimmer and may have been very different from the book published in 1912.

Let us now look at what we know about the two major poems. The essential data about *La tierra de Alvargonzález* were elucidated many years ago by Helen Grant.[11] There are three versions, all published in 1912: a version in prose published in Rubén Darío's *Mundial Magazine* in Paris, a verse form published in *La Lectura* in May and the definitive version of *Campos de Castilla*. The proximity in time of all three versions is curious; it appears that the revisions, especially of the *La Lectura* version, must be a last minute affair.

There is little doubt of the priority of the prose version, persuasively argued by Helen Grant and supported by Macrí against Carlos Beceiro,[12] and I won't go over the same ground again. Among the differences between the two versions in verse are a long semi-descriptive passage of nearly a hundred lines (ll. 183-280) added to the final version, which somewhat holds up the narrative, and a more personal note, also introduced in the final text:

> ¡Oh tierras de Alvargonzález,
> en el corazón de España,
> *tierras pobres, tierras tristes,*
> *tan tristes que tienen alma!*   (ll. 563-66)

The last two lines are added in *Campos de Castilla*, and shortly afterwards, in a line which ends the section, the repeated phase

> en el corazón de España

is changed to

> *pobres campos de mi patria.*

I must confess I find this personal intervention of the narrator intrusive. He also added the dedication to Juan Ramón Jiménez; whether he was aware or not of the incongruity involved in this is not clear.

As for *Campos de Soria*, the existence of two versions of the poem, as well as having important structural implications, raises fascinating problems of chronology which call for an explanation. Let me see if I can provide a tentative one.

First, we now have evidence of at least two stages in the composition of the poem: a first version containing the first five sections, then the twelve lines of what was later to be a separate poem, 'Noche de verano' (CXI), intercalated, and finally the famous sixth section, the invocation of Soria, with a considerable crop of variants; and the final version itself, in nine sections, with which we are all familiar.. The clear internal indication of a second visit in section VIII ('He vuelto a ver los álamos dorados') now appears to receive external corroboration. Sánchez Barbudo is right, I think, up to a point in discerning a 'tono especial de despedida' in the poem:[13] the last part has a certain quality of summing up experience and recording it memorably, but the publication history makes it highly unlikely that it was completed before the journey to France, as Barbudo suggests, for in that case he would surely have discarded the earlier version much sooner. (I am assuming, as would seem logical, that the original manuscript contained this first version). A date soon after his return to Soria in September 1911 seems the most probable time, and it fits with the 'álamos dorados' and 'hojas secas' referred to in Section VIII. Yet, in that case, why publish an outdated form of the poem so soon before its publication in book form? Not much question of a delay in printing, since a daily newspaper like *La Tribuna* is unlikely to have a long waiting list. Can a later date - March or April 1912 - and a last-minute insertion into the much delayed book be supported? - an

43

intriguing possibility indeed. The poem would then be not very distant in time from 'A un olmo seco', which dates from May 4.

Other possibilities obviously exist. The return visit, which in any case would certainly be one of many, could simply be an imaginative reconstruction rather than a specific occasion, but this goes rather against Machado's normal practice of setting out in his poems from a clear individual experience. Another possibility is that, in accordance with his habit a few years earlier, he might have handed over the first version to a friend (Juan Ramón Jiménez?) some time previously, tacitly permitting him to publish it when convenient. Given their physical separation, I doubt if this applies in this case.

My tentative solution is as follows. Machado indeed renewed, after a long absence, his beloved walks along the far bank of the Duero in Autumn 1911, and wrote a *borrador*, but not a final version, of parts of Sections VII, VIII and IX. Then, in his desire to support a new progressive newspaper in early 1912, he gave it the old version, probably already included in the Renacimiento manuscript. Doing so may perhaps have stimulated him to revise and finish the poem and incorporate it into his book at the last minute, perhaps with the final revision of *La tierra de Alvargonzález*.

The poem records a deep emotional experience, at the same time relived and recollected, at a moment when, overwhelmed with affection for the region and its inhabitants, he puts aside for the moment - if I am right - his awareness of the potential loss which he was facing in the terminal illness of his wife. It may even be that those piously exaggerated hopes he expressed for the countryfolk of Soria in the final exclamations, so distinct from the harsh reality they actually faced, correspond to a secret consciousness that neither these aspirations, nor Leonor's recovery, however fervently desired, will in fact be realized:

> ¡Gentes del alto llano numantino
> que a Dios guardáis como cristianas viejas,
> que el sol de España os llene
> de alegría, de luz y de riqueza!   (*PP*, 516)

The existence of an earlier version also throws light on the question of whether the poem is to be considered nine independent compositions or a united whole. Back in 1973, I argued in favour of unity, and saw the sixth section - the evocation of Soria - as the personal axis on which the whole poem revolves.[14] With the inclusion of 'Noche de verano', we have, not one, but two urban landscapes, with some repetition of motifs, such as the moon and the clock tower. 'Noche de verano' is evidently, as I see it, a more objective complement, without lyricism or historical connotations, of the '*Soria pura...*' section, which is the culmination of the poem in the earlier version. What happens, in my view, is that when he decides to add a personal recapitulation (sections VII-IX) echoing the earlier sections, and drop 'Noche de verano' from this composition, the '*Soria pura...*' section becomes the pivot of the poem instead of its conclusion. Furthermore, the final text significantly revises the earlier *La tribuna* version. The latter begins with four extra lines, not a vocative but a rather limp statement:

> Soria, mística y guerrera,
> de vieja estirpe cristiana,
> fue hacia Aragón barbacana
> de Castilla en la frontera.

In the earlier version 'the castillo guerrero' is 'castillo roquero', and the 'señores,/soldados o cazadores' are 'señores,/guerreros y cazadores'; 'portales' are 'portones'. More important, as Carlos Beceiro has explained (p. 1012), is the use of the second person throughout the first evocation:

> Soria fría, *Soria pura*,
> *cabeza de Extremadura*,
> con tu castillo guerrero
> arruinado, sobre el Duero;
> con tus murallas roídas
> y tus casas denegridas.   (*PP*, 514)

The established text combines skilfully, not only Soria lyrically evoked in the exclamations, but, through the third persons, all those emotionally involved with the city. Finally, the past tense is used to describe the striking of the clock: 'la campana / de la Audiencia dio la una'. The present of the final version gives the occasion greater immediacy. The changes bring into more effective focus the personal vision of a historical city full of traces of a glorious past now disappeared and of a decayed and stagnant present, in which the poet nonetheless finds beauty. I do not agree with those critics who see this description as completely negative,[15] much less with those like Michael Predmore who even suggests that 'la visión de Machado no deja de ser satírica e incluso burlona'.[16]

Now to the third grouping on the list, of poems published between 1912 and 1917. There is a notable speeding up of publications, especially in 1913, when 17 poems (counting 9 'proverbios y cantares' as one) appeared or were written. How do we account for this? In my opinion, there are two factors. The first is the anguish which produced the 'ciclo de Leonor' and gave rise, for a year or two, to a heightened sense of immediacy. In *Poesías completas* a coherent group of 12 poems constitute this cycle, which includes by any critical reckoning some of his finest poems. The second factor is a sense of urgency in facing national and political issues. It is well known that he contemplated suicide after Leonor' death, but was encouraged to continue living by the success of his book and the sense of something to accomplish.[17] His projects for books at this time are almost pathetically optimistic; he speaks in 1913 of 'tres volúmenes... casi terminados'.[18] They correspond for the most part to the heterogeneous elements which make up the final *Campos de Castilla*: 'Hombres de España', 'Apuntes de paisaje' and 'Cantares y proverbios'. All three directions are indeed cultivated, but their scope is strictly limited. The 'Hombres de España' include not only the fine 'Elogios' - to which Giner, Ortega and Azorín - with reservations - are added, but their undesirable counterparts, equally impressive as poems, 'Este hombre del casino provinciano' and 'Don Guido'. The 'Apuntes de paisaje' will include the modest success of his poems about Baeza like 'Noviembre 1913' (33; CXXIX) or the more ambitious 'Los olivos' (36; CXXXII). The most uninterrupted of his poetic veins is the 'Proverbios y cantares', which continue in *Nuevas canciones*, but there are not enough of these to form an independent book.

And there is the other side of the coin: the feeling of a drying up of inspiration which besets him, to judge by the Valcarce poem, from January 1913 onwards. He suggests two reasons for this loss. The first is the 'temptation' of the *galerías*, in which he caught a glimpse of 'el ventanal de fondo que da a la mar sombría', a temptation one would have thought to have been exorcized by the more outward-looking Castilian poems. The second is a typically elusive reference to

> ¿Será porque se ha ido
> quien asentó mis pasos en la tierra,
> y, en este nuevo ejido
> sin rubia mies, la soledad me aterra?   (*PP*, 589)

Can we doubt the eventual deleterious effect of his bereavement, which is here evoked? At the end of the poem, however, he does put some inspiration together, though it is significant that the direction it takes is towards that typical sort of martial imagery - not his best, in my view - which characterizes Machado's social involvement:

> Y cíñete la espada rutilante,
> Y lleva tu armadura,
> el peto de diamante
> debajo de la blanca vestidura.   (*PP*, 589)

At the same time, he is capable of such a magnificent poem as 'Poema de un día' (32; CXXVIII), in which he allows philosophical problems - divergent attitudes to the passing of time, his personal loss, the implications of Bergson and Unamuno - to arise naturally within the boring routine of a rainy day. It is, however, an isolated achievement. More often, one finds, in civic poems like 'El mañana efímero' (39; CXXXV), a lessening of that acute observation which was his distinctive strength. Where the falling-off becomes most noticeable is in those poems where his sense of mission has no starting point at all in observed reality, like those two lamentable twins, 'Una España joven' (48; CXLIV) and 'España, en paz' (49; CXLV). If the immediate consequence of his loss was a heightened anguished inspiration, it seems to me that the long-term effect was a disastrous break in continuity.

Finally we come to *Poesías completas* (1917). Most of its new characteristics have already been outlined: the poignancy of 'el ciclo de Leonor', the dispersed inspiration of the Baeza poems, the accentuated civic concerns, with their successes and failures, the continuation and consolidation of the folklore tendency. We should finally note the new structure. Forty more poems are added to the corpus, apart from almost doubling the number of 'Proverbios y cantares' from 28 to 54. This is accomplished, as is clear from the information I have circulated, with little regard to chronology, but rather according to a loose criterion of appropriateness, sometimes applied retrospectively, so that a poem like 'Las encinas' (7; CIII), which in fact has a wider range than the purely Sorian poems, is placed among them, as is the short evocation of the Guadarrama (8; CIV); the Leonor poems follow a clear sequence from 19 to 31, or CXV to CXXVII; the 'Elogios' are gathered together at the end, together with some poems in which the laudatory content is limited; a few poems like 'Fantasía iconográfica' (11; CVII), already in *Campos de Castilla* (1912), and 'El bufón' (42; CXXXVIII), once an 'Humorada', like the early 'Parábolas' in 1912, do not appear to fit in anywhere. The pattern adopted in 1917 is maintained, with only minimal changes, in all subsequent editions (2nd, 1928; 3rd, 1933; 4th, 1936). The canon of *Campos de Castilla* as we know it is thus completed.

NOTES

1   *Poesie di Antonio Machado*, ed. Oreste Macrí, 3rd ed (Milan: Lerici, 1969), p. 79.

2   'Precisiones sobre "Campos de Castilla" de Antonio Machado', *Celtiberia*, 64 (1982), 234.

3   Discovered by Heliodoro Carpintero, *Insula*, nos. 344-45 (July-August 1975). For a detailed study see Jorge Urrutia, 'Bases comprensivas para un análisis del poema "Retrato"', *CHA*, 304-07, (October 1975-January 1976), II, 920-43.

4   The six poems which appeared in *Revista latina*, 30 October 1907, include the very introspective LXXXVII (2nd part), LXXVIII y LXXIX. Various poems, evidently less subjective, like the five first compositions of *SGOP*, had already appeared in March 1907, and 'Orillas del Duero' (IX) was written as a result of his first visit to Soria in May.

5   *Antonio Machado, poeta de Castilla* (Valladolid: Ambito, 1984), p. 31.

6   On 24 October 1909 Villaespesa wrote to Juan Ramón Jiménez, with certain irritation, that 'Antonio apenas si hace un verso desde que se casó con la hija de su pupilera en Soria'. *Insula*, no. 149 (April 1959).

7   Arthur Terry, *Antonio Machado: 'Campos de Castilla'*, Critical Guides to Spanish Texts, 8 (London: Grant & Cutler, 1973), pp. 23-28.

8   Miguel Pérez Ferrero, *Vida de Antonio Machado y Manuel*. (Madrid: Rialp, 1947), p. 131.

9   Ricardo Gullón, 'Cartas de Antonio Machado a Juan Ramón Jiménez', *La Torre*, VII, no. 25 (1959), 185.

10   'La primera versión del poema "Campos de Soria" de Antonio Machado', *CHA*, 304-07, (1975-76), I, 1005-13.

11   'La Tierra de Alvargonzález', *Celtiberia*, 5 (1953), 57-90.

12   'La Tierra de Alvargonzález: un poema prosificado', *Clavileño*, VII, no. 41 (1956), 36-46.

13   *Los poemas de Antonio Machado* (Barcelona: Lumen, 1967), p. 206.

14   'The Unity of "Campos de Soria"', *HR*, 41 (1973), 285-96. Arthur Terry, in his excellent Critical Guide, also treats the poem as a unity (33-38), using similar arguments to mine. Sánchez Barbudo (199-207) considers the first four parts as one poem, and the fifth and sixth as distinct poems. He is followed in this by Andrew P. Debicki, 'La perspectiva y el punto de vista en poemas descriptivos machadianos', *Estudios sobre Antonio Machado*, ed. José Angeles (Barcelona: Ariel, 1977), pp.163-75.

15   See Nancy A. Newton, 'History by Moonlight: Esthetic and Social Vision in Machado's "Campos de Soria"', *KRQ*, 26 (1979), 15-24, and Gustavo Pérez Firmat, 'Antonio Machado and the Poetry of Ruins', *HR*, 56 (1988), 1-16, who treats it as an entirely independent poem on the subject of ruins.

16   Michael P. Predmore, *Una España joven en la poesía de Antonio Machado* (Madrid: Insula, 1981), p.153.

17   'Cartas a JRJ', p. 188.

18   'Autobiografía escrita en 1913', published by Francisco Vega Díaz in *PSA*, no. 160 (1965), 49-99.

APPENDIX

CAMPOS DE CASTILLA: Dates of Poems

Arabic numbers refer to *Campos de Castilla*; Roman numerals to *Poesías completas*.

1. Poems written or published before *Campos de Castilla* (1912)

56: CLII	'A Juan Ramón Jiménez' [1903?]			SGOP2;	CCI
50: CXLVI	'Esta leyenda...' [1904]			SGOP1 (1907)	
51: CXLVII	'Al maestro R.D.' [1904]	*Renacimiento*	Dec 1907	SGOP2	
55. CLI	'A D. M. de Unamuno' [1905]			SGOP1 (1907)	
1. XCVII	'Retrato'	El liberal	1.ii.1908		CCI
11: CVII	'Fantasía iconográfica'	*La lectura*	Dec 1908		CCI
40: CXXXVI	'Proverbios y cantares' ii-xi	*La lectura*	Feb 1909		CCI
13: CIX	'Amanecer de otoño'	*La lectura*	May 1909		CCI
14: CX	'En tren' [ll. 23-49]	*La lectura*	May 1909		CCI
16: CXII	'Pascua de resurrección'	*La lectura*	May 1909		CCI
40: CXXXVI	'Proverbios y cantares' i; xii-xx	*La lectura*	May 1909		CCI
2: XCVIII	'A orillas del Duero'	*La lectura*	Feb 1910		CCI
3: XCIX	'Por tierras de España'	*La lectura*	Dec 1910		CCI
8: CIV	'¿Eres tú...?' [1911]	*Nuevo Mundo*	1914		
15: CXI	'Noche de verano'	*La tribuna*	2.iii.1912		CCI
17: CXIII	*Campos de Soria* [1st version: I, II, III, IV, V, 15, VI]	*La tribuna*	2.iii.1912		CCI
18: CXIV	*La tierra de A.G.*	*La lectura*	Apr 1912		CCI

2. Poems first published in *Campos de Castilla* (1912)

4: C   'El hospicio'

12: CVIII   'Un criminal'

14: CX   'En tren' [ll. 1-22, 50-53]

17: CXIII   *Campos de Soria* [VII-IX]

40: CXXXVI 'Proverbios y cantares' xxi-xxiii
             [xxiv]: 'Eran mis dolores...' (= LXXXVI)
           'Proverbios y cantares' xxiv-xxvi; li-lii

41: CXXXVII 'Parábolas' IV, V, VII

42: CXXXVIII 'Mi bufón'

3.   Poems written or published between *Campos de Castilla* (1912) and *Poesías completas* (1917)

19: CXV	'A un olmo seco' [4.v.1912]	*El por cast*	20.ii.1913
45: CXLI	'A Xavier Valcarce'	X.V: *Poemas* (Jan 1913)	
10: CVI	'Un loco'	*El por cast*	27.i.1913
35: CXXXI	'Del pasado efímero'	*El por cast*	6.iii.1913
30: CXXVI	'A José María Palacio'	[29.iii.1913]	
29: CXXV	'En estos campos...'	[4.iv.1913]	
20: CXVI	'Recuerdos'	[Apr 1913]	
5: CI	'El Dios ibero'	*El por cast*	5.v.1913
22. CXVIII	'Caminos'	*La lectura*	May 1913
25: CXXI	'Allá, en las tierras...'	*La lectura*	May 1913
26: CXXII	'Soñé que tú...'	*La lectura*	May 1913
39: CXXXV	'El mañana efímero'	*La lectura*	May 1913
40: CXXXVI	'Proverbios y cantares' xlii-l	*La lectura*	May 1913
47: CXLIII	'Desde mi rincón' [1913]	*El por cast*	1913?
53: CXLIX	'A N. Alonso Cortés' [24.x.13]	A.C: *Arbol añoso*	1913
32: CXXVIII	'Poema de un día' [1913]	*La lectura*	May 1914
33: CXXIX	'Noviembre 1913'	*Nuevo Mundo*	1914
34. CXXX	'La saeta'	*Nuevo Mundo*	1914
7: CIII	'Las encinas'	*El por cast*	23.vii.1914
48: CXLIV	'Una España joven' [1914]	*España*	29.i.1915

43:	CXXXIX	'Elogios: ...Giner...'	*España*	26.ii.1915
49:	CXLV	'España, en paz' [10.xi.14]	*España*	26.iii.1915
46:	CXLII	'Mariposa de sierra' [28.v.15]	*La lectura*	1915?
38:	CXXXIV	'La mujer manchega'	*España*	23.ix.1915
52:	CXLVIII	'A la muerte de R.D.' [1916]	*España*	17.ii.1916
31:	CXXVII	'Otro viaje'	*La lectura*	Aug 1916
41:	CXXXVII	'Parábolas' I, II, III	*La lectura*	Aug 1916

4. Poems first published in *Poesías completas (1917)*

6:	CII	'Orillas del Duero'
9:	CV	'En abril, las aguas mil'
21:	CXVII	'Al maestro *Azorín*...'
23:	CXIX	'Señor, ya me...'
24:	CXX	'Dice la esperanza...'
27:	CXXIII	'Una noche de verano'
28:	CXXIV	'Al borrarse la nieve...'
36:	CXXXII	'Los olivos I and II'
37:	CXXXIII	'Llanto de... D. Guido'
40:	CXXXVI	'Proverbios y cantares' xxvii-xli; liii-liv
41:	CXXXVII	'Parábolas' VI, VIII
44:	CXL	'Al joven ... Ortega...'
54:	CL	'Mis poetas' [Berceo]

Questioning the Rules: Concepts of Deviance and Conformism in *Campos de Castilla*

ROBIN WARNER

University of Sheffield

It would be as well to stress from the outset that my concern here is with *Campos de Castilla* as poetry not as social document. I would contend, nevertheless, that the linked concepts of deviance and conformism underpin many of this work's specific criticisms of Spanish society. Just as importantly, they provide Machado with an effective means of raising ideological forms of thought to reflexive awareness - a means, that is to say, of bringing into the open assumptions and beliefs which are ideologically suppressed or distorted. Even a modicum of attention, moreover, to the topic of deviance can make a contribution to the relatively neglected question of the way Machado embodies a critique of social institutions and attitudes in essentially poetic forms of expression.[1]

The concept of deviance is, of course, contentious. One useful advantage its generalized scope enjoys over more restricted notions such as criminality or delinquency is that our attention is drawn to basic difficulties of definition, to the interplay of relative values across a wide spectrum of social behaviour. Such problems are wittily implied in an early (1955) definition: 'knavery, skullduggery, cheating, unfairness, crime, sneakiness, malingering, cutting corners, immorality, dishonesty, betrayal, graft, courruption, wickedness and sin - in short, deviance'.[2] More than forty years before, it is worth recalling, Machado concluded an inventory of typical Castilian inhabitants with a not, in essence, dissimilar, if shorter list:

> lechuzos y rufianes,
> fulleros y truhanes,
> caciques y tahúres y logreros. (*PP*, 591)

The problem is not simply one of variety, it is also one of legitimacy and consensus: 'Deviance does not inhere in the individual or the behaviour; it is a social judgment of that behaviour'.[3] Accordingly, if certain actions are claimed to break the rules, we might want to know where and when these rules apply, with what authority have they been made, how widely are they respected, and so on. In this sense, to ask questions about deviance is to ask questions about respectability, whereas to accept deviant labels unthinkingly is to acquiesce in a given organization of society. I hope to show that it is precisely this underlying relationship to which

Machado draws our attention. He seems not so much concerned with aberrant or conformist forms of behaviour in themselves as with the framework of social values by which they are defined.

In the prose version of *La tierra de Alvargonzález*, as a postscript to a report of the horrifying murder of a local girl, 'cosida a puñaladas y violada después de muerta', Machado proposes a series of demographic equivalences for a degenerate national obsession with deviance:

> En las pequeñas ciudades, las gentes se apasionan del juego y de la política, como en las grandes, del arte y de la pornografía - ocios de mercaderes -, pero en los campos sólo interesan las labores que reclaman la tierra y los crímenes de los hombres (*PP*, 761).

Not all the enthusiasms mentioned here may seem, at first impression, to have to do with deviant behaviour. On the other hand, readers familiar with *Campos de Castilla* will recognize that the majority of items on this list are far from innocuous. Rather than considering them as a whole, however, it may be better to begin by examining the one which is incontrovertibly concerned with serious delinquency: 'los crímenes de los hombres'.

La tierra de Alvargonzález is itself, of course, a legend of greed, murder and retribution. The same motif of parricide is given a much sharper ideological focus in the poem 'Un criminal'. This powerful composition is far from being a reworking of the 'canto romántico al reo'.[4] It carefully evokes the demeanour, circumstances and psychology of the accused man, considers the motives of his crime and comments critically on the workings of the institution whose nominal function it is to administer justice on society's behalf. We might note, to begin with, that the title suggests a certain interest in the concept of criminality, an impression reinforced by the careful avoidance of any direct description of the murder for which the man is on trial. (Such omission is in direct contrast to *La tierra de Alvargonzález*, both the verse and prose versions of which give grisly details of death-wounds.) 'Un Criminal', we might infer, is not so much concerned with exemplary or symbolic meanings of parricide, as with the way the crime is socially conditioned, defined and punished.

But what sort of cognitive-normative assumptions is Machado bringing into view here? The opening description, perhaps, provides a clue. Interest in physical characteristics is associated with the Italian Positivist School of criminology, whose ideas were well-known and influential in Europe from the last quarter of the nineteenth century onwards. Machado's criminal certainly does not have the prominent jaw, close set eyes, receding hair, tattoos and other alleged tell-tale features of the criminal type according to Lombroso's early formulations. But when we are invited to notice that

> Arde en sus ojos una fosca lumbre
> que repugna a su máscara de niño... (*PP*, 507)

parallels with the notion of atavism may come to mind. Positivist Criminology, influenced by Darwinian theory, regarded the criminal as a kind of throw-back to a more primitive stage of human development. Enrico Ferri, for instance, in a work which had appeared in several European languages by the early eighteen-nineties, adduces a 'defective resistance to criminal tendencies and temptations, due to that ill-balanced impulsiveness which characterizes children and savages'.[5]

To point to a certain congruence between such a formulation and Machado's presentation of the man on trial is not, of course, to suggest that Machado subscribed to the theory of criminal types. Nevertheless, it may be worthwhile considering the broader framework of Positivist Criminology in order to ascertain whether there are points of contact with Machado's approach in the poem as a whole. Firstly, it should be appreciated that, for Lombroso (in his later works), Garofalo and Ferri, identification of criminal predisposition was a means to an end, that of a more rational, more equitable and less crime-ridden society. In this they were consciously concerned to progress beyond both Beccarian and traditionally revanchist concepts of criminal justice. Ferri, in particular, advocated social reform ('penal substitutes') as the only effective remedy for the prevalence of criminal behaviour. As he puts it ,'up to this time, legislation and... the administration of justice has judged and punished crime in the person of the criminal, but hereafter it will be necessary to judge the criminal as well as the crime' (46). It is necessary, that is, 'to study the natural genesis of criminality in the criminal and in the physical and social conditions of his life' (xvi). Machado's poem, with its attention to the disposition of the criminal, its stress on what we now call environmental factors and its critical attitude towards social institutions, does appear to follow such an approach.

In a number of areas, in fact, the critical perspective adopted by Machado broadly coincides with that of Ferri's *Criminal Sociology*. When we read that the *acusado*, sexually frustrated and unable to marry unless he inherits his parents' farm,

> ... se acordó del hacha que pendía
> en el muro, luciente y afilada (*PP*, 508)

we recognize what the Italian School would classify as the occasional criminal, that is, the type that lacks forethought and strength of character, so that when the idea of crime presents itself it 'dwells, resists the weak repulsion of a non too vigorous moral sense and finally prevails' (43). No particular importance should be attached to Ferri's inclusion of the climate, season and soil conditions among the physical factors which have a bearing on crime, or his advocacy of 'wise testamentary legislation to prevent murders through the impatient greed of next-of-kin' (128), but we should note that his account of the influence of education on criminal tendencies is broadly in line with the values and methods of the Institución Libre de Enseñanza. Ferri warns that too much of what he terms 'archeology' can only enfeeble the pupil's sense of the actual, and that schools should offer, with far less emphasis on discipline, 'knowledge serviceable in actual life' (131). The poem certainly endorses Ferri's opinion that 'the reform of religious charities... could lead to the prevention of crime' (123-24). Given the pernicious educational role attributed to the Church in the making of Machado's murderer, 'que va sin remedio al palo', there is a certain gruesome appropriateness in the poet's denunciation, in a letter to Unamuno, of 'el lazo de hierro de la Iglesia católica que nos asfixia'.[6]

It is particularly instructive to compare positivist criticisms of the operation of criminal courts with the depressing scene evoked in the final section of the poem. In Ferri's own terms, the jury is a primitive and retrogressive institution, easily swayed by oratorical persuasiveness and sentimental declamations (192, 198). Judges are complacently guided by narrow legalistic definitions (165, 45). Barristers are engaged in 'combats of craft, manipulations, declamations and legal devices which make every criminal trial a game of chance' (164). The punitive or deterrent concept of sentencing is largely ineffectual (142), and the whole court procedure is marked by a 'hollow and superstitious formalism' (177). Machado's testimony would seem to bear out these charges:

> Frente al reo, los jueces en sus viejos
> ropones enlutados;
> y una hilera de oscuros entrecejos
> y de plebeyos rostros: los jurados.
> El abogado defensor perora,
> golpeando el pupitre con la mano;
> emborrona papel un escribano,
> mientras oye el fiscal, indiferente,
> el alegato enfático y sonoro. (*PP*, 508)

Overall, then, and although there can be no question of claiming a specific influence, it seems we should not discount the possibility that Machado was aware of and sympathetic to this widely diffused set of theories. But can 'Un criminal' be considered straightforwardly positivist in orientation?[7] The poet's less than complete faith in the value of scientific rationalism, evident in the contemporary first series of 'Proverbios y cantares', would suggest otherwise. Machado's characteristic treatment of moral issues, moreover, is hardly in keeping with the (positivist) 'belief that there is a consensus of value in society that can be scientifically ascertained'.[8]

For that matter, there are certain superficial points of contact between Machado's poem and a concept advanced by Emile Durkheim in the eighteen-nineties: anomie, the 'normlessness' which afflicts societies in which there is an in-built discrepancy between social ambitions and the means of achieving them.

> In *Suicide* [anomie] is used to characterize the pathological mental state of the individual who... suffers from 'the malady of infinite aspiration'. It is accompanied by 'weariness', 'disillusionment', 'disturbance, agitation and discontent'. In extreme cases this condition leads a man to commit suicide and homicide.[9]

Whereas the Italian Positivists associated crime with insufficiently socialized individuals, Durkheim proposed that crime should be viewed as an integral part of the way society itself is organized. Since his theories are based on conditions of life in industrialized societies, any similarity with Machado's view of rural crime should probably be regarded as fortuitous, although it can serve to warn us against a unidimensional interpretation of deviance in 'Un criminal'.

The poem, in fact, consistently touches on matters of ideology beyond the immediate topic of crime. In particular, the allusions to fatalism, to the perversion of vital energy and to the essential emptiness of institutionalized rituals and gestures are recognizable as recurrent motifs of *Campos de Castilla*. The notion of the criminal's childish or primitive lack of forethought is also relevant to what Machado sees as a generalized national propensity. Indeed, perhaps the most forceful aspect of the poem as ideological critique is the way it exposes a complacent or ignorant acceptance of what is, a conformism which rules out analytical reflexion or appreciation of the need for change. Nor does the provinciality of the setting limit the scope of Machado's criticism, since the backwardness of rural areas serves to expose the general malady of Spanish society with particular clarity: 'desde estos yermos se ve panorámicamente la barbarie española y aterra'.[10] A similar perspective, perhaps, informs the poem 'Un loco', where the pathetic eponymous figure is set in a rural landscape which is thematically contrasted with a morally degenerate urban environment. The unhappy man himself is presented as the expiatory victim of 'un pecado ajeno', the sins, presumably, of so-called normal society.[11]

At this juncture it is necessary to leave the relatively uncomplicated area of clearly defined delinquency and consider the paradoxical notion of deviant conformism. A number of poems in *Campos de Castilla* invite the reader to recognize that deviance is structurally embedded in normal society, that the dominant system of values is itself reprehensible. As Machado remarks in the tenth of his 'Proverbios y cantares', it is vice, not virtue, that is envied by present-day Cains (*PP*, 570), an insight into topsy-turvy morality echoed in the proposal to Unamuno that 'tendremos que rectificar algo más que conceptos: sentimientos, que nos parecían santos y que son, en realidad, criminales, inhumanos'.[12] One of Machado's most effective strategies for bringing his readers' attention to bear on this issue is to highlight examples of what could be termed tolerated deviance, that is, activities which are officially proscribed but in practice are permitted and even admired.

Wide-spread connivance in electoral fraud, essential to the operation of the 'turno pacífico', is specifically mentioned by Machado in 'Poema de un día' and 'Del pasado efímero'. Less obvious examples of tolerated deviance are provided by 'Los olivos', a poem often praised for its positive evaluation of ordinary working people. Their worth is enhanced, it is worth noting, by contrastive allusions to aberrantly non-productive life-styles. Leaving aside the poem's closing condemnation of religious seclusion, we might note two references to officially deprecated ways of life:

> ¡De la venta del camino
> a la puerta, soplan vino
> trabucaires bandoleros! (*PP*, 561)

> ¡... los benditos labradores,
> los bandidos caballeros,
> los señores
> devotos y matuteros! (*PP*, 562)

The reference to dealing in contraband, an activity which is not only unproductive but actually has an adverse effect on the national economy, has a particular relevance in a country which had tended to favour protectionist trade policies.[13] Banditry, equally detrimental to society, occupies an even more anomalous position between official condemnation and popular fascination and even approval. As such, it is included among the dubious activities which alone can rouse some semblance of enthusiasm in the dreary figure who represents 'el pasado efímero':

> Sólo se anima ante el azar prohibido,
> sobre el verde tapete reclinado,
> o al evocar la tarde de un torero,
> la suerte de un tahúr, o si alguien cuenta
> la hazaña de un gallardo bandolero,

o la proeza de un matón, sangrienta. (*PP*, 559)

As for the remaining items in this list of degenerate inclinations, one is reminded of Ferri's remark that 'the prohibition of cruel spectacles and the suppression of gambling houses are excellent penal substitutes' (131). The references to bullfighting in this poem (and in others) suggest that Machado regarded the popularity of 'la fiesta nacional' as evidence of backwardness and emptyheadedness; the characterization of traditionalist Spain as 'devota de Frascuelo y de María' in 'El mañana efímero' comes particularly to mind. The references to gambling, however, form part of an even more systematic critique of the national mentality.

Organized gambling represents a clear case of tolerated deviance. It was made illegal in the Criminal Code of 1848, a prohibition that was confirmed in that of 1879. Machado was probably aware of the controversy which accompanied an unsuccessful proposal, in 1912, to introduce controlled legalization. But the law in any case was widely flouted. As one legal historian has remarked:

> Este panorama de prohibición sin duda no fue nunca muy efectivo en realidad - ni aún por parte de las autoridades... ni en la condena social, de tal modo que este género de delincuencia estaba prácticamente inédito, siendo poca la jurisprudencia existente de fines del siglo pasado y comienzos de éste.[14]

In 'Del pasado efímero' Machado's mention of the technical illegality of gambling does not, apart from the obvious institutional debility implied by infraction, seem to go beyond a strong suggestion that the activity is attractive precisely because it is unlawful and precisely because it is both easy and safe to indulge in it. Not for this character the rebellious commitment to deviance which expresses criticism and rejection of the normal. His gambling is perfectly in keeping with the outlook of his youthful counterpart:

> al estilo de España especialista
> en el vicio al alcance de la mano. (*PP*, 567).

The image of the gambler bent over the table, his eyes firmly directed downwards, links his attitude to life both with that of the accused in 'Un criminal', who 'conserva del obscuro seminario... la costumbre / de mirar a la tierra' (*PP*, 507), and, more importantly, with that of the misguided worshipper in 'El Dios Ibero':

> con mi oración se inclina
> hacia la tierra un corazón blasfemo. (*PP*, 497)

In this poem, in fact, we find Machado's most systematic use of the motif of gambling to highlight fatalistic acceptance of what is an ideologically conditioned blindness to any notion of the future as the product of conscious human agency rather than chance, prevalent in a society condemned elsewhere as

> ... un pueblo impío
> que juega al mus, de espaldas a la muerte. (*PP*, 593)

'El Dios Ibero' makes the link between gambling and perverted religious beliefs absolutely explicit. The opening lines of the poem recall the traditional anecdote of a 'ballestero tahúr' who attempts to revenge himself on God for his bad luck by shooting an arrow into the sky, and the grotesque prayer which takes up much of the poem is described as 'un dado de tahúr al viento'. Machado's treatment of religious issues is a topic too complex to analyse in any depth here, although it is worth pointing out that not only does Machado tend to present religious beliefs (or lack of genuine ones) as a model of national ideology in general, but also that he often invites the reader to consider the link between devotional norms and propensities to deviance or delinquency. To the examples already noted we might add some of the piously conformist Don Guido's youthful bad habits, or the character of the typical 'hombre de estos campos':

> Abunda el hombre malo del campo y de la aldea,
> capaz de insanos vicios y crímenes bestiales,
> que bajo el pardo sayo esconde un alma fea,
> esclava de los siete pecados capitales. (*PP*, 495)

'El Dios ibero' provides a particularly powerful example of such a synthesis. Reverence for God, 'dueño de la nube del estío', is characterized as the farmer's blasphemously superstitious obsession with the success or failure of his crops. The deeper ideological implications of such an attitude are then pointed up by further references to games of chance:

> ¡Oh dueño de fortuna y de pobreza,
> ventura y malandanza,
> que al rico das favores y pereza
> y al pobre su fatiga y su esperanza!
> ¡Señor, Señor: en la voltaria rueda
> del año he visto mi simiente echada,
> corriendo igual albur que la moneda
> del jugador en el azar sembrada! (*PP*, 497)

In this blending of slavish obsession with material success or survival, degenerate forms of worship and unquestioning acceptance of the social status quo, the motif of gambling serves to emphasize the extent to which 'el hombre ibero' has renounced his human birthright of reflexion and meaningful action. He is incapable of any consensual attempt to make the future, but, like the gambler at the roulette wheel, can only put his faith in chance to enrich him at the expense of his fellows.

It may now have become apparent that Machado's inclusion of obsessive concern with the land in the list of deviant propensities given in the opening pages of *La tierra de Alvargonzález* is by no means inapposite. Indeed, when we read the first lines of 'Por tierras de España',

> El hombre de estos campos que incendia los pinares
> y su despojo aguarda como botín de guerra ... (*PP*, 495)

and realize that the oft-evoked barren landscapes are the consequence of a characteristically improvident policy of tree clearance, the relevance of land reclamation to a broader deficiency of outlook is unmistakable. As Machado angrily demands in 'Nuestro patriotismo y la marcha de Cádiz':

> ¿Llamaréis patria a los calcáreos montes, hoy desnudos y antaño cubiertos de espesos bosques, que rodean esta vieja noble ciudad? Eso es un pedazo de planeta por donde los hombres han pasado no para hacer patria, sino para deshacerla.[15]

Against such a view of short-sighted toil directed to narrowly self-interested goals, Machado sets a concept of constructive work, that is, cooperative activity to prepare the ground for a better future.

> Para salvar la nueva epifanía
> hay que acudir, ya es hora,
> con el hacha y el fuego al nuevo día. (*PP*, 594)

The linked motifs of axe and fire are not, therefore, associated exclusively with thoughtless destruction. It is true that it is a wood-cutter's axe which often serves as an instrument of murder or as a symbol of wasteful death - one thinks here not only of *La tierra de Alvargonzález* and 'Un criminal', or the fate of the 'olmo seco', but also of the bereaved old man in *Campos de Soria*, sitting in the firelight with his

> ... hosco ceño,
> como un tachón sombrío
> - tal el golpe de un hacha sobre un leño -. (*PP*, 514)

Netherthless, in 'El mañana efímero' or the chiding 'envío' of 'Desde mi rincón', as well as in the references to 'leña verde' and 'pura llama' in 'El Dios Ibero' the same motifs serve to symbolize purposeful national regeneration.

Such an apparent paradox seems typical of Machado's approach to the issues I have considered here. As a caring member of a society whose dynamism is shackled by ossified ideologies, his strategy is to problematize them, and thus engage the reader in a process of thought and debate about genuinely desirable values. Notions of deviance are particularly susceptible to such a treatment, since not only are they heavily infiltrated by ideological prejudices, but these in turn are relatively easy to pinpoint because of their practical manifestations. To put this another way, we could say that a delinquent is a stereotype, but he is also, in practice, an individual in a social context, a locus of specific referents which can provide material for figurative discourse. More importantly, perhaps, the processes by which the delinquent (or the conformist) is stigmatized (or legitimized) as such are embedded in forms of social communication, and especially in language. For the creative writer, and particularly, it could be argued, for the poet, there is considerable scope here for ironic dialogue with official or standardized discourses. To give one pungent example, Machado describes his criminal as 'devoto de María, / madre de pecadores' (*PP*, 507). Poetry is a medium well suited to effects of this sort, since the reader of a poem is keenly aware of each word and phrase unfolding as a counterpoint to existing or potential utterances. As Claudio Guillén has pointed out (although his approach derives from formulations of Jakobson rather than Bakhtin) this pointedly dialogic quality is of particular relevance to elements of social criticism in *Campos de Castilla*.[16]

There is thus a potential for ideological commentary in the very matrix of poetic utterance. The effect of implicit dialogue with standardized forms of discourse is often to reclaim for evaluation assumptions that otherwise remain ideologically suppressed. Thoughtlessly habitual attitudes and the complacent reiteration of 'sagradas formas y maneras' (*PP*, 568) are brought into critical consciousness. In *Campos de Castilla*, it is often the notion of deviance which is employed to catalyze such a re-ordering of perspectives. Habitual drunkenness, to take a marginal yet instructive example, can certainly be viewed as an infringement of social norms. But, in the angry extended metaphor of the bad wine in 'El mañana efímero', Machado condemns not rule-breaking, but the degeneration which results from lazily hedonistic improvidence:

> Como la náusea de un borracho ahíto
> de vino malo, un rojo sol corona
> de heces turbias las cumbres de granito;
> hay un mañana estomagante escrito
> en la tarde pragmática y dulzona. (*PP*, 568)

In drawing attention in this thought-provoking way to notions of aberrant behaviour, Machado is asking his readers to reject the easy option of reducing complex social issues to conventional moral categories and attributing them exclusively to stigmatized individuals or groups. In short, he is asking them to recognize that it is just such ideological labelling that stands in the way of consciousness, consensus and action to remedy serious national problems. To remain, for a final moment, with the drink problem, we find a powerfully clear example in 'Una España joven' of the way Machado can problematize concepts of deviance to set his readers questioning the mechanisms of ideological conditioning and social control:

> ... A España toda,
> la malherida España, de Carnaval vestida
> nos la pusieron, pobre y escuálida y beoda,
> para que no acertara la mano con la herida. (*PP*, 594)

NOTES

1   Although the presence of a 'socio-ideological' dimension in *Campos de Castilla* is generally accepted among critics, there has been relatively little analysis of it in terms of poetic procedures. For an account of approaches and problems see Robin Warner, 'Critical Reports. Ideology and Expression in Machado's "Campos de Castilla"', *Neophilologus*, 73 (1989), 230-42.

2   Albert Cohen, quoted in Jack Douglas and Frances Walker, *The Sociology of Deviance* (Boston: Little, Brown and Co., 1982), p. 8.

3   P. Conrad and J. Schneider, *Deviance and Medicalization* (St. Louis: Mosby, 1980), p. 6.

4   As has been claimed in a fairly recent critical survey. See A. Fernández Ferrer, *Antonio Machado: Campos de Castilla* (Barcelona: Laia, 1982), 52.

5   Enrico Ferri, *Criminal Sociology*, ed. W.D. Morrison (London: Fisher and Unwin, 1895), p. 11. Subsequent page references are to this work. I was unable, unfortunately, to consult the Italian original, but, in any case, it is the broad influence of this type of theory rather than of any particular text that is at issue here.

6   *Poesía y prosa*, III, p. 1536.

7   John Crispin, for instance, comes very close to such a view when he considers the treatment of the similar crime in *La tierra de Alvargonzález*: 'Machado insiste primero en el progreso material y socio-político'. '"La tierra de Alvargonzález" como alegoría noventayochista', *Insula*, nos. 344-45 (July-August 1975), 14-15.

8   Jock Young, 'Thinking Seriously about Crime: Some Models of Criminology', in M. Fitzgerald, G. McClennan, J. Pawson (eds.), *Crime and Society* (London: Routledge, 1981), p. 269.

9   Stephen Lukes, 'Alienation and Anomie', in P. Laslett and W. Runciman (eds.), *Philosophy, Politics and Society* (Oxford: Basil Blackwell, 1967), quoted and discussed in D. Downes and P. Rock, *Understanding Deviance* (Oxford: Clarendon, 1982), p. 95.

10   *Poesía y prosa*, III, p. 1519.

11   The madman thus represents a clear example of deviance imposed on an individual by the values of 'normal' society - unfortunately, this poem raises too many complex issues of interpretation to be considered here in detail.

12   *Poesía y prosa*, III, p. 1558.

13   In the view of some economic historians, the effects of such policies in the crucial cereals sector was a root cause of the lack of dynamism whose manifestations Machado consistently attacks. See Gabriel Tortella, 'La economía española a finales del siglo XIX y principios del siglo XX', in J. L. García Delgado (ed.), *La España de la Restauración* (Madrid: Siglo XXI, 1985), pp. 133-51.

14   Luis López Torrubia, 'Economía del juego', *I.C.E.* (May 1983), 37-42.

15   *Poesía y prosa*, III, p. 1484.

16   Claudio Guillén, 'Proceso y orden inminente en "Campos de Castilla"', in José Ángeles (ed.), *Estudios sobre Antonio Machado* (Barcelona: Ariel, 1977), pp. 195-216.

Poeticidad en *La tierra de Alvargonzález*

ROBERTO A. VALDEÓN

University of Glasgow

La principal dificultad que uno se puede encontrar a la hora de hacer un análisis de alguna obra de Antonio Machado es la amplia difusión que el poeta ha tenido durante todo el siglo, tanto dentro como fuera de España, tanto a nivel de su obra como de los comentarios a que ha dado lugar.

Por otro lado la situación política que vivió España tras la guerra civil hizo posible una mayor difusión de su poesía como hombre republicano, exilado y muerto en Francia, que servía de ejemplo a todos aquellos que continuaban la lucha desde el interior. Al mismo tiempo, la España de la posguerra llevó a cabo una curiosa tarea de 'rescate' del poeta, como señalaré más adelante.

Sin embargo no todo se ha dicho y probablemente nunca se diga sobre su obra, una obra rica, llena de matices, de sentimiento y sobre todo de poeticidad. Es en este punto donde se va a incidir en esta charla: la poeticidad en la obra de Machado a través de *La tierra de Alvargonzález*.

Suele aludirse a Machado como un poeta sencillo, esencialmente bueno, claro, transparente. Estos adjetivos han ido con frecuencia muy unidos a él. Desde sus primeros estudiosos hasta los más recientes parecen sentir un gusto especial al referirse a Machado como el poeta bueno por excelencia. Pero esto, sin dejar de ser cierto, no forma parte sino de su intimidad, que sin duda se refleja en el conjunto de su obra. Pero esta está dotada de otras características. Los árboles no dejan ver el bosque. La sencillez desbordante no ha permitido ver y descubrir su cuidada composición, sus versos escogidos, sus figuras estilísticas. Aunque también es cierto que otros críticos han intentado valorar con justicia la creatividad en la obra de Machado. Así Cesare Segre lleva a cabo un interesante trabajo sobre lo cuidada que está cada palabra en la obra de Machado, aunque haga mayor referencia a *Soledades*.[1] Sin embargo he elegido una de sus obras en *Campos de Castilla*, por ser este libro al que más afecta el calificativo de sencilla, por ser una obra emblema frente a la España de la posguerra y de los opositores al régimen, y porque en cierto modo está necesitada de un proceso de rehabilitación, que la incluya más como literatura que como un panfleto de una lucha política, por otro lado muy legítima, una vez que se haya restituido su valor como obra literaria.

En efecto ese cariz de hombre bueno que afectaba a don Antonio, y por ende a su poesía, fue utilizado tras la guerra por los hombres adictos al régimen para llevar a cabo lo que fue denominado un rescate. Así Dionisio Ridruejo (luego opositor a Franco, como sucedería con tantos otros intelectuales que creyeron en Franco como la mejor solución a los males de España) escribía un curioso prólogo tras la guerra civil, en el cual, basándose en la calidad de hombre de bien de Machado, lo rescataba de las filas de la masonería, ya que (siempre según Ridruejo) esa condición había sido la que le había inducido a formar parte del bando de los perdedores y era necesario rescatarle de aquel secuestro intelectual: el *propagandista propagandeado* fue la definición que le dio.[2] De la misma forma observaba Ridruejo en Machado todas las características de un hombre preocupado por España y por lo tanto de un verdadero patriota. De nuevo la obra de Machado era utilizada desde una óptica extraliteraria, y en este caso inclusive deformadora. Sin embargo, ante todo, Machado es poeta. Su obra, poesía.

Veamos el motivo por el cual se ha elegido *La tierra de Alvargonzález*. En realidad existen varios motivos para elegir esta obra:

(a)   Supone una obra lo suficientemente amplia dentro de *Campos de Castilla* como para hacer un análisis sobre ella sin romper la unidad de la misma.

(b)   Es un caso único dentro de la obra de Machado, porque se trata de un romance, es decir un experimento, por llamarlo de alguna manera, que no repetiría.

(c)   Mantiene la atención del lector fija en la historia que se narra con lo que no se presta mayor atención a la poesía.

La obra forma parte de *Campos de Castilla* (1912) y existe una versión escrita en prosa con anterioridad. El propio Machado dijo al respecto:

> Me pareció el romance la suprema expresión de la poesía y quise escribir un nuevo Romancero. A este propósito responde *La tierra de Alvargonzález* (...). Mis romances no emanan de las heroicas gestas, sino del pueblo que las compuso y de la tierra en donde se cantaron; mis romances miran a lo elemental humano, al campo de Castilla y al Libro Primero de Moisés, llamado Génesis.[3]

Por ser el romance una historia, parece lógico pensar que los procedimientos utilizados van a hacer de la misma una narración poética, más que poesía por sí sola. Ciertamente el carácter de la historia va a influir decisivamente en su forma externa. Pero más bien a su favor que en su contra: la necesidad de acoplar una narración corta al ámbito poético estimula la creación de una estilística propia que mantenga un preciso equilibrio entre dicha narración y su forma poética consiguiente. En este sentido podemos hablar de una 'poeticidad narrativa', pero dejando bien claro que ninguno de los dos términos subordina al otro. Es decir que no se trata de forzar la trama a favor de la forma, ni de distorsionar la forma poética a favor de que la trama mantenga su claridad.

Comienza *La tierra de Alvargonzález* con un planteamiento de la situación de partida y que se desarrollará después. El punto de partida no puede ser más significativo:

> Siendo mozo Alvargonzález,
> dueño de mediana hacienda,
> que en otras tierras se dice
> bienestar y aquí, opulencia... (vv. 1-4)

Prestemos mayor atención a los dos últimos versos. No son una combinación producto del libre albedrío, ni mucho menos. Diferencia radicalmente el concepto de riqueza que se tiene en Castilla y por extensión en toda España con respecto a la de otras tierras, posiblemente Europa. Esta simple diferenciación consistente en dos versos está dotada de unas connotaciones que no podemos pasar por alto:

(a) Lleva a cabo un proceso de condensación de significados en tan sólo dos versos. Las implicaciones son claras: el estado de retraso de España frente al resto de Europa es tal que incluso la riqueza se mide por distintos parámetros. De forma muy hábil asegura que en otras tierras se llamaría bienestar y aquí se llama opulencia. Dos diferentes connotaciones según España y Europa. El significado de las palabras varía según la situación del país. Sobre el tema, otros podrían escribir ensayos, a Machado le sobran sólo dos versos.

(b) Como consecuencia de ello, descubrimos su inclinación noventayochista, que le hace renegar de lo que él denomina 'La España de charanga y pandereta'. Esta preocupación por la miseria de España, típica de los hombres del 98, aparece reflejada en el romance constantemente, pero es en estos dos sencillos versos donde adquiere su mayor significación, porque es donde esa dicotomía adquiere los tonos dramáticos que auguran el resto de la trama. Es decir, no son fruto de un azar, sino que su situación al comienzo de la obra suponen un aviso al lector de que esa diferenciación va a ser a la postre trágica.

Se trata, pues, de una dicotomía de trágicas consecuencias. El motivo principal aparece en el propio texto: la diferente consideración que adquieren las tierras en un lugar y otro no significa que ambas sean correctas. Más bien parece inferirse lo contrario: el término que elige el poeta, 'mediana hacienda', parece aproximarse más a 'bienestar' que a 'opulencia'. No es que Machado esté dándonos información gratuita o irrelevante. Nos ofrece pistas de los acontecimientos futuros; el hecho de que Castilla tenga un sistema de valores diferente al de otras zonas es sintomático de su tragedia. Es este sabio proceso de selección lo que llama nuestra atención en el romance de Machado: la cuidada selección de palabras.

En efecto la carga de connotaciones que conllevan algunos versos nos indican su poeticidad. No en vano, los versos más famosos de toda la obra sean los que demuestran su desgarrado lamentar por España:

> Oh, tierras de Alvargonzález,
> en el corazón de España,
> tierras pobres, tierras tristes,
> tan tristes que tienen alma!   ('La casa', II, vv. 41-44)

y concluye 'La casa' así:

> ¡Oh pobres campos malditos
> pobres campos de mi patria!   (vv. 53-54)

Son quizá estos versos la culminación de la obra. En ellos queda patente el sentimiento del poeta al escribirlos. Sin duda, la preocupación le desborda. Y dentro de esa desesperación, otorga alma a los campos o tierras. Por lo tanto el alma va unido a un sentimiento de tristeza, de pobreza, de soledad. Pero cabría preguntarse el motivo de esta unión entre alma y pobreza. Se trata, sin duda, de expresar un sentimiento de pesar, de dolor. El recurso del que se vale nos resulta inesperado. Lleva a cabo un proceso de reflexión y nos ofrece dos palabras como expresión verbal del mismo. Ambas forman parte del discurso habitual del español y ambas admiten diferentes connotaciones en diferentes contextos. Sin embargo Machado las utiliza con un fin muy particular, y, por lo tanto no admitirían cualquier significado. Existe un punto en el que esas dos palabras convergen. En esa intersección encuentra el poeta la expresión de su sentimiento, el momento en el que lo pobre y lo triste vienen a formar parte de un mismo concepto. Ese concepto queda completamente definido por el segundo verso: la posesión de alma. Por ese motivo se puede decir que los campos tienen alma, porque comparten esas dos citadas características. Más adelante veremos como los hermanos mayores participan en menor grado de esta pobreza, pero eso no les permite tener alma. En todo caso, no el alma que Machado otorga a los campos.

Veamos en qué sentidos la asociación de palabras es efectiva con respecto al lector:

(a)   Comunica su propio estado de preocupación e impotencia.

(b)   Invita al lector a compartirlo, a no ser un mero receptor de sentimiento, y a reflexionar sobre ello. La sencillez de la exposición poética deja paso a una reflexión compartida. La forma es sencilla, pero la poeticidad ha alcanzado cotas de participación mucho más amplias.

(c)   Por otro lado existe una razón inmanente: la necesidad de entroncar con un sentimiento más profundo y sincero hacia esas tierras y que quizá de otro modo no se consiguiese, o al menos no completamente.

Por lo tanto tenemos un sentimiento de pena por España, que se traduce concretamente en Castilla y sus campos, y que se nos presenta nada más comenzar el romance. A lo largo de la obra se vuelve a desarrollar y se retoma de forma gloriosa (para el poeta y para nosotros) en la segunda parte de lo que titula 'La casa'.

Sin embargo podría pensarse que estos dos grupos de versos son contradictorios, ya que en un primer momento expresa un sentimiento de pena que le lleva a otorgar alma a los campos, al relacionarlos con la tristeza que parece ser la tónica general de los mismos, mientras que en el segundo bloque asegura que los pobres campos están malditos. Cabría preguntarse si de alguna forma la segunda parte no anula la primera, ya que una maldición parece dominar esos campos (y por lo tanto a sus habitantes). No obstante ello no tiene por qué ser así. Machado nos proporciona nuevos datos en la valoración de los campos. Hay un doble plano 'material/espiritual' que divide 'la maldición' por un lado y 'la tristeza-el alma' por otro. La primera es un producto de esa situación particular a la que nos referíamos más arriba: status diferente, personajes diferentes (y personajes que no comparten los mismos ideales sobre las tierras que poseen: ello ha de reflejarse más adelante en la ambición sin límites de los hijos mayores que los lleva al asesinato). La segunda es un producto de la anterior, es decir que las tierras sufren de la naturaleza de sus poseedores o pobladores, lo que las convierte en tierras pobres y tristes, para finalmente otorgarles alma.

La importancia de los personajes en el texto es indudable. Son cuatro: el padre, los dos hijos mayores y, finalmente, el hijo menor (el indiano). Los papeles que desempeñan en la obra son fundamentales. El padre (Alvargonzález) y su hijo pequeño son la bondad del campo. Los dos hijos mayores representan la codicia, la maldad. Nos encontramos con esta nueva dicotomía, un tanto maniqueísta. Sin embargo, nada está tomado a la ligera y los cuatro cumplen funciones clave: el padre es el amor a la tierra, las buenas tradiciones, es la fusión ideal entre tierra y dueño, de la que resulta una confusión de los términos 'poseedor' y 'poseída'.

Como también lo es su hijo menor, a pesar de haber colgado la sotana. Con respecto a los dos hermanos mayores ya todo es distinto: son la clara representación de la codicia, de la sangre de Caín, de las tradiciones obsoletas, del mal vivir. Son, en suma, la representación de la 'España de charanga y pandereta', la España de opereta.

Por lo tanto y, conocida la importancia del tiempo en la obra de Machado, padre e hijo menor están situados cronológicamente antes y después de los dos hermanos mayores: son la esperanza muerta, asesinada y la nueva esperanza.

Ello queda corroborado en ejemplos como:

> Feliz vivió Alvargonzález
> en el amor de su tierra ... (vv. 17-18)

En estos versos comprobamos lo antes dicho: la unión entre campesino y tierra resulta ser de amor. Alvargonzález vivió feliz junto a su familia y sobre todo amando a su tierra. Existe una evidente personificación de la misma. En este aspecto existen en la obra de Machado rasgos idealizantes que contribuyen y fomentan la poeticidad de la misma. En efecto *La tierra de Alvargonzález* muestra un cierto influjo platónico al considerar las ideas de bien y bondad paralelas a la de belleza. Las ideas de justicia, belleza y bien como cima del mundo inteligible. Además el Sol era el símbolo de las tres pues proporciona luz, vida y calor a los seres.

Paradójicamente, o no tanto, la importancia del sol en esta obra es también grande. Así en la primera parte de 'La casa' se puede leer:

> Cuando en brazos de la madre
> vio la figura risueña
> del primer hijo, bruñida
> de rubio sol, la cabeza... (vv. 57-60)

Es decir la idea de sol va unida a la de la ingenuidad de la infancia, aunque con el tiempo se transforme en codicia.

Así mismo el color blanco viene a simbolizar la pureza del hermano menor, y cuando este regresa a casa, aparece cubierto de blanca nieve:

> .. Venía
> todo de nieve cubierto...   ('El viajero', III, vv. 3-4)

Junto a esa idealización externa de la bondad y el bien, nos encontramos con la idea de belleza como ya habíamos señalado con anterioridad:

> De los tres Alvargonzález
> era Miguel el más bello
> porque al mayor afeaba
> el muy poblado entrecejo
> bajo la frente mezquina,
> y al segundo, los inquietos
> ojos que mirar no saben
> de frente, torvos y fieros.   ('El viajero', IV, vv. 21-28)

La belleza externa del pequeño no es otra que una exteriorización de su belleza interna, del bien y la bondad que van parejos por dentro.

No es ni mucho menos un antojo inútil, un capricho de poeta. La pertinencia de la definición de los hermanos tal como aparece es comprensible. Forma parte de la simbología de la obra, que permite 'lecturas al sesgo'.

Apreciamos esta simbología por el desarrollo de la historia en el romance, que siendo una historia en el tiempo, trasciende de algún modo lo puramente temporal e inclusive lo meramente espacial, para hacerse extensible a otros momentos y otros ámbitos más amplios. La estructura es, sin duda, interesante.

La situación inicial es de equilibrio, por lo tanto de felicidad. A esta situación sigue una ruptura producida por la codicia de los hijos. La ruptura tiene un reflejo en un plano irreal (el sueño) y en un plano real (el asesinato). Como consecuencia de esa ruptura nos encontramos frente a la infelicidad, la tragedia, el crimen. Al avanzar la historia tenemos el arrepentimiento interno de los dos personajes, que se materializa en su proposición de olvidar el pasado y para ello utilizan los medios a su alcance: la vuelta al hogar del hermano menor, el indiano. La situación de desequilibrio se repite, puesto que la codicia surge de nuevo. Y el punto final es el castigo.

70

Hasta ahora hemos tratado de relacionar cada personaje con la función que cumple dentro del poema: Alvargonzález es el equilibrio inicial, los dos hermanos mayores la codicia, la envidia y por lo tanto el desequilibrio. Y finalmente Miguel (el indiano) es un digno sucesor de su padre, con todos los calificativos idealizados que antes se han señalado.

Quizá por ello cree Manuel Alvar que, en *La tierra de Alvargonzález*, el poeta linda lo evangélico.[4] Machado utiliza personajes humanos, claros y sencillos (como tantas veces se ha dicho), pero si bien se podría indicar que Machado simplemente lleva a cabo un proceso de valoración de la historia que narra y que por lo tanto ello le da licencia de utilizar elementos que considere oportunos dentro de la creatividad poética que requiere (y que no tiene por qué tener límites), también es cierto que el poeta parece utilizar repetidamente episodios bíblicos en la composición de su historia. De todos ellos el más obvio es la referencia a la sangre de Caín que corre por las venas de los hermanos mayores. Pero no se trata de una simple referencia, puesto que los hermanos acabarán con la vida del padre y más adelante volverán a sentir la tentación tras el regreso de Miguel, con lo cual se repite la utilización de un episodio bíblico y, en este caso, resulta más evidente pues se relaciona con el hermano.

No ha de resultarnos extraño el hecho de que Miguel sea el hermano pequeño y que además haya tenido una vocación religiosa. Sin embargo Miguel abandona los latines y decide que no quiere vestir por la cabeza, pero ello no quiere decir que Miguel haya perdido su fe, ni mucho menos, como suele pasar con otros hombres en su misma situación, Miguel sigue del lado de Dios. Tan sólo ha perdido fe en la institución, en la Iglesia. Lo corrobora su éxito en ultramar, su triunfal vuelta al hogar (sólo sus tierras producen, mientras que las de sus hermanos quedan sumidas en un invierno interminable) y finalmente el hecho de que Miguel parece estar protegido contra el 'hacha de guerra' de sus hermanos.

Por otro lado el mero regreso, la vuelta al hogar nos recuerda la parábola del hijo pródigo del Antiguo Testamento.[5]

Por lo tanto, como señala Manuel Alvar, no se trata de contar, de narrar, relatar, sino más bien de interpretar y valorar. La poesía lo hace perfectamente. De nuevo Alvar señala que 'los recursos de que se vale, apenas si nos permiten un mínimo asidero. Y sin embargo rara vez en nuestra poesía se habrá encontrado un testimonio más claro y más auténtico'.

De acuerdo con la segunda parte, no así tanto con la primera, y en los siguientes puntos de análisis vamos a tratar de demostrar que Machado sí que utiliza una retórica, es la apropiada para la historia. No una retórica pobre, más bien cabría decir que otros autores utilizan una retórica demasiado rica.

No responde Machado a la tradición española de forma categórica: se mantiene prudente, como bien se observa en esta obra, en la que la tradición nos viene dada a través del personaje de Alvargonzález. Refleja esta tradición en versos como:

> Naciéronle tres varones,
> que en el campo son riqueza,
> y, ya crecidos, los puso,
> uno a cultivar la huerta,
> otro a cuidar los merinos,
> y dio el menor a la Iglesia. (vv. 19-24)

De nuevo encontramos resumidos en los últimos tres versos de los citados una muestra de la poeticidad siempre implícita en su obra. Estos tres versos son una calificación y una definición de lo que España ha sido a través de su historia: un pueblo agrícola y ganadero ('la huerta' y 'los merinos') y un pueblo íntimamente ligado a la Iglesia: 'y dio el menor a la Iglesia'. Una tradición de siglos apoya este último hecho. No obstante esta defición puede referirse más concretamente a Castilla, región menos desarrollada que otras periféricas dentro de España. Pero bien es verdad que Machado, como otros hombres de su generación literaria, consideraba que Castilla era la fiel representante de los males de España. Es decir, ha logrado resumir en tres versos siglos de historia.

Machado adopta una actitud crítica en los dos aspectos:

En el fragmento siguiente comienza así:

> Mucha sangre de Caín
> tiene la gente labriega,
> y en el hogar campesino
> armó la envidia pelea. (vv. 25-28)

Si la tradición de España se encontraba en el campo, paralelamente sus males también lo están ahí. La alusión es clara y directa, no ofrece la menor duda: a través de una antítesis entre los fragmentos II y III del comienzo, Machado nos ofrece la cara y la cruz de la vida campesina: la felicidad y la codicia, fruto de la falta de evolución y el anquilosamiento.

En el mismo fragmento se encarga Machado de la otra parte de la tradición: la Iglesia. El hijo menor había sido entregado a la Iglesia (durante siglos ello fue así entre las principales familias). Pero Machado nos dice que esto no es bueno, pertenece al pasado, a un pasado poco grato. Machado, prudente, atribuye el abandono de la profesión eclesiástica a las doncellas primero:

        El menor, que a los latines
        prefería las doncellas
        hermosas...   (vv. 37-39)

Da la impresión de que Miguel es demasiado frívolo para seguir una carrera eclesiástica, sin embargo a renglón seguido se hace más explícito:

        ... y no gustaba
        de vestir por la cabeza,
        colgó la sotana un día...   (vv. 39-41)

Es interesante señalar que el poeta utiliza dos versiones para justificar el mismo hecho: las doncellas y la falta de convicción. Pero no parece probable que ambas sean compatibles con el posterior desarrollo de la historia. Más bien habría que pensar que Machado hace uso de un recurso que utilizará con frecuencia a lo largo de todo el poema: la transcripción de los murmullos de la gente, de la razón que encontraron los habitantes del pueblo para que dejara los latines. Conociendo la sangre de Caín de la gente labriega, es fácil reconocer que la noticia del abandono de la carrera eclesiástica por parte de Miguel habría de suponer un pequeño escándalo, más aún cuando se nos ha dicho que pertenece a una familia relativamente importante dentro de la comunidad y cuyas vidas estarían frecuentemente en boca de todos. Con esta situación de fondo no es difícil suponer que las malas lenguas pronto inventarían una historia en torno al abandono. Esa historia es la que nos ofrece Machado al principio. Sin embargo el poeta también desea incluir una razón más seria, quizás la auténtica, que Miguel no gustaba 'vestir por la cabeza'.

Hay que señalar el sútil empleo que Machado hace de dos preciosas metonimias: los latines y la sotana, elementos que definen al clérigo (quizá más entonces que ahora), son utilizados para hacer referencia a la propia profesión, más que vocación. Con los latines se refiere a los años de estudio, de aprendizaje; con la sotana se refiere al momento en que esos años de estudio produce unos frutos visibles en la indumentaria y en el status de la persona que se ha entregado a esta vida.

Por lo tanto y resumiendo:

(a)   Ha hecho un compendio de historia y tradición en tan sólo tres versos.

(b)   Ha rechazado ambas con pruebas irrefutables.

73

(c)   Todo ello lo hace con admirable sutilidad, utilizando contraposiciones y dos
bellas metonimias.

El tema de la tradición continuará más adelante siguiendo una tónica muy parecida. Así
en el fragmento IV de 'Aquella tarde...' se puede leer:

> Un buhonero, que cruzaba
> aquellas tierras errante,
> fue en Dauria acusado, preso
> y muerto en garrote infame.   ('Aquella tarde', IV, vv. 9-12)

Tras el asesinato de Alvargonzález, vilmente cometido por sus hijos, otro hombre es
acusado y muerto a garrote infame. Ahora lo que se pone en tela de juicio es el sistema de
justicia (o injusticia) imperante, así como su medio último para llevarla a cabo: el garrote vil.
De nuevo la condensación es perfecta: en cuatro sencillos versos se ha expuesto y se ha
valorado, negativamente por supuesto. La sustitución del término 'vil' por 'infame' no es
tampoco arbitraria, ni mucho menos. Aparentemente son dos sinónimos, sin embargo la
utilización de 'infame' supone la valoración del propio autor al respecto. El propio Alvar
señala que la colocación del adjetivo en Machado no es arbitraria. Estas palabras habría que
completarlas diciendo que, en realidad, se trata de una sabia reflexión.

Paralela a la tradición y con algunos puntos confluyentes, la codicia es el motor que
mueve a los hermanos. En realidad forma parte de lo que podríamos denominar como 'el
quinto personaje', que va unida al asesinato, la muerte, la envidia y todas las imágenes que
Machado utiliza para referirse a ellas: la luna, la noche, los cuervos, la laguna que todo lo calla.

Ya hemos visto como en el comienzo del fragmento III de la primera parte se nos
presenta:

> Mucha sangre de Caín
> tiene la gente labriega...   (vv. 25-26)

Esta nueva metonimia (se cita al malvado por excelencia, Caín, para relacionarlo con
sus dos dignos sucesores: los dos Alvargonzález mayores) es un nuevo ejemplo de esa
capacidad de condensación de que Machado hace gala.

Por lo tanto los calificativos aplicados a los dos hermanos mayores son, hasta ahora,
envidiosos, feos y malos; la pobreza completa el cuarteto:

Así a un año de abundancia
siguió un año de pobreza   ('Castigo', I, vv. 7-8)

y al año pobre siguieron
largos años de miseria.   ('Castigo', II, vv. 11-12)

No tan sólo una pobreza material, sino una que trasciende al espíritu de los personajes. Habíamos visto que Machado había otorgado alma a aquello que ya tenía pobreza ('Tierras pobres'). Sin embargo en este caso la diferencia es sustancial. En aquel primer caso 'pobres' estaba unido al adjetivo 'tristes' y esto daba lugar a una nueva valoración del primer adjetivo, que nada tiene que ver con su utilización en solitario. La unión de adjetivos delimita el significado hasta el punto de formar un todo indisoluble, puesto que han confluído en una zona de intersección: aquel punto en el que la unión de ambos produce un significado que no podrían tener por separado: tristes y pobres, de lo que se deriva que tienen alma.

Sin embargo, los hermanos son pobres, no tristes, sino cobardes. De esta forma el adjetivo 'pobres' se vacía del contenido que tenía anteriormente y se llena de otro mucho más peyorativo: míseros, resultado de una miseria interior que no puede producir la existencia de alma en ellos.

De esta forma nos hallamos ante un ejemplo de la sencillez de Machado, producto de una búsqueda ardua: una palabra ('pobreza') se encuentra en una unidad mayor (en una antítesis o en una redundancia), que a su vez forma parte del concepto de castigo y éste a su vez del concepto-base de codicia: una sucesión de paréntesis.

Junto a la tradición y a la codicia, es patente un elemento misterioso en el romance, un elemento esotérico. Podría tratarse de un componente meramente estructural: algo parecido a lo que ocurre en las leyendas románticas de Bécquer con las que tiene algunos puntos de contacto. Pero mientras en las *Leyendas* es un componente enmarcado dentro del movimiento romántico (exotismo, misterio, retorno a lo medieval), dos pueden ser los motivos para el empleo de lo misterioso, elemento que aparece reflejado en tres momentos clave:

(a)   El sueño y el asesinato: la Laguna Negra.

(b)   El agua que extiende la culpabilidad de los hermanos por la zona.

(c)   El castigo final a manos de la Laguna Negra.

En primer lugar recordemos unas palabras de Gabriel García Márquez con respecto a su obra y más en concreto con respecto a *Cien años de soledad*. El autor colombiano aseguraba que en una historia siempre hay dos versiones: una la verdadera y otra la leyenda que el pueblo teje en torno a la primera.[6] El asegura que prefiere siempre la segunda. Este camino es el que parece elegir Machado: elige la leyenda misteriosa en lugar de la realidad cruenta y vulgar. Opta por un lirismo que la poesía refleja mucho mejor que la narración. Es un paso más hacia la poeticidad, porque mejor que ningún otro género la poesía es capaz de expresar 'lo sobrenatural sin sobresaltos'.

En los tres últimos fragmentos (IV, V y VI) de 'Los asesinos' y del romance confluyen todos estos aspectos misteriosos y sobrenaturales hasta el punto de crear pánico en los dos hermanos, miedo en el lector No vamos a repetirlos todos, pero es conveniente ver algunos ejemplos:

> aquí bocas que bostezan
> o monstruos de fieras garras...   ('Los asesinos', IV, vv. 7-8)

> Era la noche, una noche
> húmeda, oscura y cerrada.   ('Los asesinos', V, vv. 3-4)

> Cien ojos fieros ardían
> en la selva, a sus espaldas.   ('Los asesinos', V, vv. 7-8)

Pero con dejar claro lo importante del elemento misterioso, resultan más significativos estos dos versos:

> En el hondón del barranco
> la noche, el miedo y el agua.   ('Los asesinos', IV, vv. 15-16)

En este caso la conjunción de nombres que llevan implícito un mismo estigma provocan la premonición de la muerte.

En segundo lugar la utilización de Machado de la versión que podría correr de boca en boca, la versión misteriosa y popular, puede ser una forma de atacar el fuego con el fuego: emplea la superchería popular para llevar a cabo la venganza, o más bien la justicia a través de la Laguna Negra.

Lo primero que nos llama la atención al descubrir un poema de Machado en *Campos de Castilla* es la plasticidad pictórica con que se describe los campos y las tierras castellanas. Ello forma también parte de *La tierra de Alvargonzález*, en la que además encontramos una descripción de las estaciones paralela.

La parte titulada 'Otros días', compuesta de cinco diferentes fragmentos, nos lo muestra claramente. Son las descripciones de Machado descripciones llenas de alma y de espíritu, como la misma tierra que contempla y plasma. Y lo hace aplicando toda suerte de colorido y ello mediante los adjetivos. Sus descripciones no serían lo mismo sin los adjetivos, porque captan, dibujan, condensan y por lo tanto llevan a cabo un acoplamiento de lo adjetivado. No podría decirse que Machado pinte poesía, pero sí que escribe una poesía pictórica. Impresionista, quizá, porque nos ofrece retazos más que cuadros perfectamente acabados. Al menos ésta es la opinión de Alvar. Yo, en cambio, no diría que es completamente impresionista, porque Machado no descompone para volver a componer, sino que compone sobre lo ya existente, sobre lo que les es dado, mediante un proceso de selección personal:

> El cielo está azul, los montes
> sin nieve son de violeta.   ('Otros días', I, vv. 13-14)

En estos dos versos la descripción es perfecta, porque se supera a sí misma como palabra y porque supera lo meramente pictórico: ningún cuadro podría expresar lo que ahí aparece. Fijémonos que para referirse a la situación hace uso de nombres y adjetivos muy sencillos: cielo, azul, montes, nieve, violeta. Y el verbo es atributivo. Sencillez. Sin embargo los dos versos lo superan: expresan la situación del buen tiempo a través de la ausencia de la nieve. El adyacente negativo 'sin nieve' es el mejor medio de definir la situación, por oposición. Por lo tanto la poeticidad se logra gracias a lo que no podrían expresar los pinceles: se capta la luminosidad del día por la ausencia de la nieve.

Pero la descripción colorista del campo cumple otras funciones. Hemos comentado con anterioridad la idealización de los hermanos, una idealización en torno al bien (en el caso del indiano) y otra en torno al mal (en el caso de los dos hermanos mayores). La descripción de los campos va a contribuir de manera decisiva también en esa configuración. En el segundo fragmento de 'Castigo' puede leerse:

> pudrió el tizón las espigas
> de trigales y de avenas...   ('Castigo', II, vv. 3-4)

Estos dos versos son la consecuencia 'misteriosa' del asesinato. Si los asesinos eran pobres, malos, feos y envidiosos, el ámbito en el que se mueven no lo es menos, porque con el personaje del padre (siempre presente a pesar de su ausencia), se va la esperanza.

Sin embargo la llegada de Miguel hace abrir nueva esperanzas. Machado lo resalta así:

> Ya con macizas espigas,
> preñadas de rubios granos,
> a los campos de Miguel
> tornó el fecundo verano...   ('El indiano', I, vv. 13-16)

Junto a ello va unida la sensación de luminosidad que provoca el verano. Contribuyen al colorido, la luminosidad:

- la abundancia de epitetos
- la utilización de términos con connotaciones que hacen referencia al color dorado, muy unido al paisaje de Castilla, aquí estilizado. Así, por ejemplo: *verano, sol, espigas, rubio, dorado, oro*, etc.
- la conjunción de sustantivos o adjetivos con esa intención selectiva a la que ya nos hemos referido.

Es, pues, el paisaje por sí mismo o por su relación trascendente a los personajes y su distinción entre el bien y el mal, aspecto decisivo de esta obra, como lo es en general en toda su poesía.

Hasta ahora hemos visto como se poetizan temas amplios como la preocupación por España, la codicia, la tradición, la idealización, el bien y el mal. También aspectos más concretos como el paisaje y el colorido. Pero existen además cuatro elementos más concretos.

La Laguna Negra, las aguas, la noche y el camino son símbolos y formas muy precisas, con las que nos encontramos en cada fragmento. Pero son también elementos muy comunes a otras obras, en las que utiliza los mismos símbolos para expresar la misma preocupación. Son, en definitiva, otra contribución a la poeticidad de la obra machadiana.

Muchos son los caminos que el poeta trazó a lo largo de su vida, muchos los que anduvo (el más penoso, sin duda, el de su exilio) y es lógico que conociera los distintos caminos del mundo. En este obra, el camino que aparece es la muerte. Alvargonzález 'anduvo largo camino' para llegar a la muerte y también lo anduvieron sus dos hijos mayores para llegar al mismo destino. Los asesinos utilizan un camino para huir, y por un camino pasaba el pobre buhonero al que matan con 'garrote infame'. Cuando los asesinos toman un camino siempre parece llevarles a un destino con connotaciones negativas. Así en 'Otros días', cuando cogen un camino para ir a comprar ganado, se encuentran desamparados. Cualquier camino de esperanza está lejos de los hermanos, todos son para ellos caminos de terror, noche y muerte.

78

La simbología del camino no está perfectamente definida. Ahora bien, va relacionada con la tierra y con los asesinos. Al cometer el asesinato, los hermanos se ven aprisionados por esa tierra que ansiaban. Los caminos que salen de ella sólo llevan una dirección: la muerte. Permanecer en las tierras es una muerte lenta, una muerte en vida. Intentar salir, huir por alguno de los posibles caminos es salir a buscar la muerte. Por lo tanto el camino es un nexo entre la vida y la muerte que no deja lugar a opción. De nuevo el contenido poético viene dado por el concepto, más que por la forma. Señalemos algunos versos referidos al camino:

> iba triste y pensativo
> por la alameda dorada;
> anduvo largo camino
> y llegó a una fuente clara.   (vv. 53-56)

Una vida entera es ese largo camino, además del camino material por el que Alvargonzález pasea:

> y, camino de hayedo,
> se vio un reguero de sangre.   ('Aquella tarde', IV, vv. 3-4)

El camino comienza a teñirse de muerte:

> largo camino nos queda.   ('Otros días', V, v. 22)

El camino comienza a hacerse pesado e insoportable:

> En el hondón del barranco
> la noche, el miedo y el agua.   ('Los asesinos', IV, vv. 15-16)

Finalmente el camino lleva a la muerte. En definitiva el camino en *La tierra de Alvargonzález* no es un accidente geográfico, o una arteria entre pueblo y pueblo. Es un signo fatal que conlleva una evolución, cuya finalidad es la muerte.

La presencia del agua se da en dos campos diferentes: la de las aguas que corren, como una fuente, el 'agua que va saltando', etc. Y por otro lado, la Laguna Negra.

Ya nos hemos referido al estudio que Cesare Segre realiza sobre *Soledades* y como se centra principalmente en 'la fuente'. Cree este crítico que la fuente y, en general, el agua es una incitación al recuerdo y al mismo tiempo un testigo mudo.

En efecto la fuente es testigo mudo de la muerte de Alvargonzález:

> y a la vera de la fuente
> durmió el arrullo del agua.   (vv. 59-60)

> A la vera de la fuente
> quedó Alvargonzález muerto.   ('Aquella tarde', III, vv. 1-2)

Pero en algunos versos posteriores, las aguas 'hablarán', cuentan lo que ha sucedido. En cierto modo, no es más que un eufemismo de la realidad: los murmullos de las gentes del pueblo, que imaginan lo que ha pasado. Pero ya señalamos antes que Machado emplea aquí la versión no real, es decir que las aguas son las que extienden la tragedia:

> El agua, que va saltando,
> parece que canta o cuenta:
> "La tierra de Alvargonzález
> se colmará de riqueza,
> y el que la tierra ha labrado
> no duerme bajo la tierra."   ('Otros días', V, vv. 43-48)

El agua adquiere facultades para hablar (elemento misterioso e irónico a la vez), es personificada (recurso estilístico) y sustituye al murmullo de la gente (proceso de selección entre realidad y ficción). Tres ámbitos para lograr la poeticidad.

Paralelamente se cuenta con la presencia del agua en otro sentido: la Laguna Negra. De ella sí se puede decir que es un testigo mudo y así la define:

> y en la laguna sin fondo
> que guarda bien los secretos...   ('Aquella tarde', III, vv. 15-16)

> Llegaron los asesinos
> hasta la Laguna Negra
> agua transparente y muda...   ('Los asesinos', VI, vv. 1-3)

La pasividad de estas aguas contrasta vivamente con 'el agua que va saltando', que hemos visto antes. La quietud, la calma de estas aguas 'quedas', de estas aguas muertas, que no corren, que no toman parte de la vida, nos sugieren la laguna de *Los ojos verdes* de Bécquer, que lleva al protagonista a la muerte. Pero a diferencia de la leyenda romántica, la laguna forma parte de una visión trágica y fatalista en *La tierra de Alvargonzález*:

> y el sondarla inútil fuera,
> que es la laguna insondable.   ('Aquella tarde', IV, vv. 7-8)

La definición viene dada de nuevo por los aspectos negativos de lo descrito: 'lo insondable' es lo que la caracteriza. En ella no se puede encontrar la esperanza, es la fatalidad de la muerte, unida a la noche, a 'la luna llena, enorme globo'. Y es así como encontramos la muerte: un equilibrio entre lo temporal terreno y la atemporalidad, entre lo relativo y lo absoluto. Este zig-zag entre las aguas que saltan y la laguna quieta contribuye a ello.

Y ya para concluir, con cierto atrevimiento, voy a hacer uso de otro de los poemas machadianos::

> Da doble luz a tu verso
> para leído de frente
> y al sesgo. (*PP*, 640)

Es lógico pensar que dentro de ese mundo de simbología y poeticidad que el poeta ha trazado en torno a su obra, surja la posibilidad de una lectura 'al sesgo' o más de una. Sin embargo en la obra parecen estar claros muchos aspectos.

Podríamos encontrar en la descripción angustiosa de las tierras castellanas una angustia vital por la pobre herencia histórica y social con que España contaba:

> pobres campos de mi patria. ('La casa', II, v. 54)

A Alvargonzález le corresponde representar el papel de la España en su vertiente tradicional propiamente buena, que es asesinada por la mala, es decir por sus hijos. Sería la España de principios de siglo XX, sumida en la felicidad de pasadas glorias (los campos) y el temor a un futuro incierto (el camino por el que nuestro personaje va triste y pensativo, preocupado). De los hijos de Alvargonzález, dos representan la codicia, la envidia, llevan la sangre de Caín, entre ellos reluce un hacha de hierro. El pequeño cuelga la sotana, rompe con la 'España de charanga y pandereta' y se aleja, se abre a un nuevo mundo, distinto. De ese mundo, vuelve con una idea de cambio, de superación y de esfuerzo. Pero en su empeño, choca de nuevo con la envidia y la codicia, con sus propios hermanos. Finalmente se deja una puerta abierta a la esperanza, aún cuando el desencanto siga presente.

NOTAS

1   Cesare Segre, *Crítica bajo control* (Barcelona: Planeta, 1970).

2   Dionisio Ridruejo, 'El poeta rescatado', prólogo a *Poesías completas* (Madrid: Espasa-Calpe, 1940).

3   *Poesía y prosa*, III, p. 1594.

4   Manuel Alvar, 'Estudio introductorio' a *Poesías completas*, (Madrid: Espasa-Calpe, 1977).

5   Lucas 15:11.

6   Gabriel García Márquez, introducción a *Cien años de soledad*, (Madrid: Espasa-Calpe, 1982).

The Three *Caballeros*: Don Guido and his Relations

NICHOLAS G. ROUND

University of Glasgow

That Antonio Machado's reputation as a poet should stand high is in no sense surprising. It is much more remarkable that it should have done so ever since his lifetime, virtually unimpaired by shifts of ideology or fashion. Here, very evidently, we have something which stands in need of further explanation. If ever a poet might have been expected to become a non-person in the cultural landscape of the early Franco years, that poet was Antonio Machado. But it did not happen.[1] Three purportedly complete collections of his poetry, a substantial anthology, and reissues of three early volumes kept his work before the Spanish public between 1941 and 1949. Significantly, the earliest of these 'complete' poems carries a preface by Ridruejo entitled 'El poeta rescatado'. The essays, articles, and other substantial treatments of Machado published in Spain between the start of the decade and the massive commemorative *Cuadernos Hispanoamericanos* of 1949 total something over thirty - and if much of this work is ephemeral, some of it is not: the names of Carlos Clavería, Dámaso Alonso, and José María Valverde figure in that list. A later generation's impatience with the established monumentality of the men of 1898 is succinctly enough embodied in the title of Joan Fuster's polemic *Contra Unamuno y los demás*. But one could not readily imagine a volume of essays entitled *Contra Antonio Machado y los demás*.

Even this, however, is not the core of the matter: there have been other writers whose stature specifically as writers has been no less consistently accepted. Machado's almost exact contemporary Yeats is a case in point. But the example of Yeats only serves to define Machado's uniqueness more sharply. To later Irish writers Yeats has proved both an inescapable and an unassimilable cultural presence; his achievement has been experienced, above all, as an incentive to do something different. And it could be argued that readers too can best approach him with a similar resistance and a similar wariness. Resistance and wariness are not what Antonio Machado evokes; rather he has seemed supremely accessible and, in some especially immediate sense, available. He himself wrote of Berceo under the title 'Mis poetas', and it is in that kind of relation that he has been adopted - or perhaps *rescatado* - by all sorts and conditions of readers.

We might look for various levels of explanation of why this should be so. It is certainly not trivial to recall that the poet was remembered by those who knew him as a person of great sweetness and integrity, but it is harder to say how such matters impinge on the processes of reading and writing. On the latter Ricardo Gullón makes an observation which seems central to one important tradition in the valuing of Machado: 'Mallarmé y Neruda se apartaron con ostentación de las normas lingüísticas y de la simbología de uso general o epocal; Machado no. Su ruptura con lo uno y con lo otro es tan sutil que apenas se ve'.[2] Even here we are not far away from the domain of a more personal, biographical judgment. Gullón echoes in form, and perhaps in intention too, Rubén Darío's portrait of Antonio: 'Su mirada era tan profunda / que apenas se podía ver'. The way of seeing is registered as profound, the way of expression as subtle; but both are detected, as it were, at vanishing-point, against a background of self-effacing plainness.

It is worth reminding ourselves at this point that this is by no means the distillation of Machado's own self-assessment: the subject of 'Retrato' or of 'Poema de un día' shows no inclination to vanish. There are, of course, the heteronyms, but their function too is more positive: Juan de Mairena is perhaps a mask but hardly a refuge for his author. The subtlety and the profundity are authentically present in these items as in others, but they are not so delicate as to deprive the selves there presented of all definition or purpose. If it comes to that, the Antonio Machado of history, while remaining no less the 'Don Antonio el Bueno' of so much first-hand testimony, had purposes of his own, which he pursued with some tenacity. These were not exclusively ends of a public and historical kind. But it is among critics disposed to acknowledge and honour that aspect of Machado's development that they are most explicitly recognized: by Manuel Tuñón de Lara, for example, insisting that Machado's humanism 'nada tiene que ver con una ideología del conformismo, con esa "ética de la resignación" con tanto tino criticada por Tierno Galván'.[3] Written in 1966, this comment seems to obey two important and still valid perceptions about Machado. First it is made clear that 'humanism' will be an inescapable category in the evaluation of his work and of its tenacity of appeal. Secondly and just as clearly, it is going to be a tricky category to handle.

It has grown trickier since. Certainly the very cautious, resistant, residual quality of Machado's humanist claims gives them a greater survival-value in our own captious times than broader, more emphatic affirmations might enjoy. To invoke Yeats just once more, it is as if, every time Plato's ghost sang out its 'What then?', that modest rhetoric - so convincingly the rhetoric of an actual modesty - simply passed over the invitation to state its own case, replying merely 'Yes, indeed; but... what now?' Yet a vision and a set of linguistic strategies so tentatively advanced that each element 'apenas se ve' might well prompt another response altogether. That response would see the humanist meanings in Machado (or indeed any possible meanings in Machado) as made and unmade by his readers - the poet supplying only the texts that enable this to happen. There is a great deal in the early poetry especially which tends to corroborate this: some of the poems in *Galerías*, for example, seem positively to solicit that kind of reading. And, of course, it would chime perfectly with the theoretical canons of the moment. If this is, in fact, the way we all do read Antonio Machado, it would supply a very convincing explanation of his unique 'availability' as a poet. What it would not explain at all - indeed, it would leave the problem rather worse - is why Antonio Machado should be thus available, rather than any other poet.

I want to suggest here that something rather different is the case: that Machado's poetry is both purposive and textually open: both interpretative of experience in an identifiably intentional way, and available as an experience to readers of very different intention. In that it is perhaps not radically different from other poetry, or indeed from other language; its uniqueness lies in the particular way which it finds of being these disparate things simultaneously. We might well want to express that in the terms in which the closing lines of 'Poema de un día' provisionally define the human self: the Machado poem too seems to be 'contingente y libre, a ratos,/ creativo, original...' (*PP*, 558). To which we should add that the Machadian text, like the Machadian self, has its being from a world of otherness: other selves, other texts. It will be useful, therefore, in illustrating how all this is so, to invoke the evidence of the kind of reader who can most confidently be expected to make fresh meanings - and to unmake old ones - in the text which is being read. My point of departure, then, will be a woman reader and writer, herself engaged in composing a poem which appears to have a specifically feminist dimension of its own.

In the introduction to a volume of essays on women in Hispanic literature which she edited in 1983, Beth Miller discusses that dimension of the poem 'Caballero' by the Mexican Lázara Meldiú.[4] Accessible information about Lázara Meldiú is not easily come by. Her name does not appear in José Luis Martínez's *Literatura mexicana del siglo XX*, or in Gabriel Zaid's *Omnibús de la poesía mexicana*. She is not listed among Costa Amic's *Cien poetas mexicanos*, and no poem of hers makes an appearance among the 1020 items in Salvador Novo's *Mil y un sonetos mexicanos*.[5] Yet Lázara Meldiú was something more than a candidate for a *Cancionero apócrifo*, a 'poeta que pudo existir'. Her real name was María de la Luz Lafarja de Cruz (of which her pen-name is a partial anagram), and she was born in the province of Vera Cruz in 1902. A poet from a very early age, she had published several volumes by the mid 1940s: one of these was revolutionary and political in its inspiration, but her more characterisitc themes were those of personal feeling. Relatively late in life she produced a novel with an 'Indianist' background, *Nacu-Xanat*, published in Mexico in the 1960s. Her work appears in anthologies of Latin-American women's poetry such as Natalia

Gamiz's *Mujeres de América* and Etelvina Villanueva y Saavedra's *Ronda femenina de América*.[6] But she is not featured among Carmen Conde's *Once grandes poetisas americohispanas* or even discussed in the introduction there, though Rosario Castellanos, who rather similarly mingled lyric poetry with Indianist fiction, does receive some attention. On the evidence of the poem which Beth Miller cites, and of the handful of anthology pieces which I have managed to see, this may well be something of an injustice.

Miller herself makes strong and circumstantial claims for 'Caballero' as an example of 'underground women's poetry'. In default of any fuller biographical background one cannot begin to assess how apt that description might be. The form and diction are certainly not 'underground'; they are in the main flow of a tradition of well-wrought, consciously public poetic statement. That tradition, its lines laid down by Darío and his contemporaries about the turn of the century, continued to be available to Latin-American writers - latterly, it is true, as something rather conventional - for perhaps a generation or two thereafter. It is probably appropriate in this context to give some special emphasis to other women writers in the same mode: Delmira Agustini (another poet admired by Miller) would be one such example. If Lázara Meldiú's poem has remained 'underground' in the sense of being neglected, it is because the currents of critical fashion have driven it there. But such currents have their own determinants, still often unexamined. Part of the explanation in this case may very well be that the defiance and the irony in 'Caballero' - so obvious once Beth Miller has pointed them out - have escaped the attention of a male-dominated taste, making the poem seem less remarkable altogether than it is:

> Por tu gesto que marca la grandeza
> singular y elegante de tu raza;
> por tu perfil que tiene la serena
> línea de envejecida aristocracia.
>
> Por la callada plenitud que lleva
> la señorial sonrisa de tu hidalga
> estirpe, que jugó aventuras
> y es regia y monástica y pirata.
>
> Por tu ademán que tiene la magnífica
> tranquilidad del fraile y del monarca,
> por esa rancia lírica que forma
> la flor de los escudos de tu heráldica.
>
> Abro mi canto en madrigal de seda
> bajo la luna en madrigal de plata,
> y llego a tus deseos en ofrenda
> con un trino de alondras en el alma.

Only a very complacent masculinity indeed, we might think, could take this piece to be three stanzas of celebration of all that is brightest and best in Hispanic *machismo*, plus one stanza of predictable surrender to it. But such complacencies abound, and 'Caballero' exploits them with real skill. The elaborately wrought hyperbole of the first twelve lines brings the surface-content into question at every stage; the self-possession of the final quatrain dangerously negates the overt message of self-surrender. In that sense perhaps the 'real', feminist poem is indeed underground - the sub-text to its own acquiescent topsoil. And yet we cannot really leave the matter where Beth Miller leaves it, with talk of the 'decoding of male-poet cliches' and the exploration of 'ways to "de-create", rejecting and/or reinterpreting myths and images of women and men in literature'. We cannot leave it at that because of the existence of another poem - Antonio Machado's 'Llanto de las virtudes y coplas por la muerte de don Guido' (*PP*, 563).

There can, it seems to me, be very little doubt that Lázara Meldiú here owes a great deal to Machado's poem. Circumstantially this is perfectly credible. Don Guido made his appearance in the greatly expanded *Campos de Castilla* of 1917, and was thus almost certainly available to readers in Mexico well before Meldiú wrote 'Caballero' (which certainly does not read like an example of the poet's *juvenilia*). There is some evidence too - the topic would bear further investigation - that Machado was an important writer for several Latin-American *poetisas*. Concha Espina's interest is well-known; Dora Isella Russell wrote an essay on Machado's Civil War poetry.[7] In the few poems of Lázara Meldiú herself which I have been able to see, there are images which run parallel with those of Machado: the proletariat advancing is seen as travelling on 'Viejos caminos de piedra'; more interesting perhaps is the use of *anclar* in a love-poem, one of whose stanzas reads:

> No he pensado en anclarme todavía,
> en el poniente se tiende la promesa
> de una tierra mejor'.[8]

None of this, of course, is at all conclusive; the case of 'Caballero' and 'Don Guido' is a very different matter.

It should perhaps be made clear at the outset that Lázara Meldiú's debt to Machado is very much the kind of debt which one poet can properly owe to another, and that it in no way detracts from the achievement of 'Caballero' as a poem. What has caught the Mexican poet's attention - as Machado clearly meant to happen - is the final incongruous picture of that stylish old sinner playing the part of a devoutly Catholic corpse - 'tan formal', laid out there in his tertiary's robe. The 'fina calavera' becomes the 'perfil', losing by the way the Machadian pun on *la calavera* ('skull') and *el calavera* ('rake'). It gains a rich ambiguity of its own, however,

87

from the phrase 'envejecida aristocracia': who exactly is over the hill in Meldiú's poem, one wonders - the lineage? or the individual? or both of them together? The Machadian 'yertas manos en cruz' supply the hieratic 'ademán'. Don Guido's 'tosco sayal', like his membership of the 'santa cofradía' promotes the image of a commingled secular and sacred authority: 'regia y monástica', 'del fraile y del monarca'. But where Machado allows himself a snort of derision at the sheer brazen-necked effrontery of this assumption of the best of both worlds ('¡aquel trueno!'), Meldiú insinuates a third term, apter to the Caribbean than to the Andalusian context: 'regia y monástica *y pirata*'. There are other reminiscences: 'jugó aventuras', besides linking with the *conquistador* motif, harks back to Don Guido's unregenerate youth:

> de mozo muy jaranero,
> muy galán y algo torero...

The 'escudos de tu heráldica' are not far removed from his 'blasones' and talk of the 'tradiciones de su casa'. Significantly, these resemblances are at once compelling and elusive. They are not usually matters of verbal identity; they work much more through concepts and sound-patterns, and through the ironic placement of what purports to be a language of valuing. Compare 'tan formal' with 'la grandeza/singular', or 'la magnífica/tranquilidad' with 'la fina calavera'. In other words, Meldiú has not, precisely, imitated the Don Guido poem, but neither has she subverted it in quite the way that Beth Miller's references to de-creation and de-coding would imply. She has, to a remarkable degree, trusted what was there in the Machado text - not merely Machado's perceptions, but quite major aspects of his actual way of perceiving. Yet that has not inhibited her from absorbing and recreating these elements for independent, albeit still related, purposes of her own.

Machado's poem, then, was characteristically available to Meldiú. But it was still available very much as itself, not as a blandly adaptable text, waiting to be furnished with whatever characteristics of meaning she might choose. Nothing, of course, could be more familiar in literature than this process whereby the reading of one poem contributes to the writing of another. Indeed, that had happened already, in the composition of the 'Don Guido' poem itself. If the egregious Don Guido is the Andalusian cousin of Meldiú's 'Caballero', the two have a somewhat more distinguished ancestor. The distinction has to be queried because the record of that potentate of the Moorish frontier, Rodrigo Manrique, Master of Santiago and Count of Paredes, was itself a long way from being uniformly exemplary.[9] But that did not deter his son, the poet Jorge, from his attempt to vindicate Rodrigo's life and deeds by linking them with values which he envisaged as universal. The outcome - Manrique's 'Coplas por la muerte de su padre' - was one of the great meditative poems in Spanish (or indeed in any language). Antonio Machado admired it to the point of reverence:

> Entre los poetas míos
> tiene Manrique un altar. (*PP*, 470)

That declaration and the critical tribute in the '"Arte poética" de Juan de Mairena', (*PP*, 698-700) are only the two most obvious testimonies.[10]   The Don Guido poem, in its title, in phases of its metrical patterning, and in its theme of *hidalguía* travestied, explicitly and ruthlessly guys the object of that reverence.

In fact, the relationship between Don Guido and Manrique's 'Coplas' is more complex than that - more complex, indeed, than has sometimes been assumed.   The 'Coplas' - undoubtedly present in Machado's poem - are not self-evidently its point of departure or its central preoccupation. As Francisco López Estrada among many others has pointed out, the poet was producing a number of pieces at this time which highlighted with a certain 'humor negro' the inadequacies and falsities of Andalusian life: the 'hombre del casino provinciano' of 'Del pasado efímero' is surely a near-relative of Don Guido.[11]   Machado's letters to Unamuno contrast Baeza, with its 'población rural, encanallada por la Iglesia', unfavourably with Soria: 'Es infinitamente más levítica y no hay un átomo de religiosidad'.   And yet, as he gloomily reflects, 'esto es España más que el Ateneo de Madrid'.[12]   We can by no means rule out the possibility, Aurora de Albornoz very reasonably argues, that a real Don Guido - could his name have been Don Gil or Don Diego, one wonders? - lived, and perhaps died, in or around Baeza at about the material date.[13]   However, she assigns the further definition of this figure to other literary sources, noting Unamuno's association of the Don Juan archetype with the *señorito* who, late in life, abandons the 'caza de doncellas', marries money, and joins the conservative establishment: 'Oye misa diaria, pertenece a varias cofradías y abomina de cuantos no respetan las venerables tradiciones de nuestros mayores'.   Unamuno's essays on the subject date from 1907 and 1908, a few years before Machado's poem, but the latter's growing closeness to Unamuno in the Baeza years, together with the quite strong verbal echoes, suggest that there is something in Albornoz's view.   It is less clear, though, that it is the Tenorio association alone which ties Don Guido to Seville: as a birthright member of that city's progressive intelligentsia, Machado had his own score to settle with Sevillan *señoritismo*.

Another preoccupation of his in these years was the death of Francisco Giner de los Ríos, early in 1915; both Helen Grant and Tuñón de Lara regard the 'Coplas por la muerte de don Guido' as an ironic *contrafecha* of Machado's elegy for Giner.[14]   The tinny churchbells and the creative ring of anvils, the falsity against the authenticity, the hollow silence after '¿qué llevaste?', contrasted with the rich assurance that Giner at least had something to take with him - 'lleva quien deja...' - all lend support to this. Above all, perhaps, there is the Andalusian dimension: 'este señor de Sevilla', against 'aquel otro señor de Ronda'. Yet none of these alternatives succeeds in displacing Manrique from his relevance to the poem. The point about Giner is that his memory, like that of Rodrigo Manrique - though now without the claim to a supernatural afterlife - 'nos dexó harto consuelo'[15]; the point about Don Guido is that his does not. And the allusion of the poem's title seems unmistakable.

In fact, it is capable of being mistaken and it usually is. Only the latter half of Machado's title actually echoes Jorge Manrique; the 'Coplas' are never presented as a *llanto de las virtudes*. There is another Castilian poem of the same period which does bear that title, and a very fine one it is too; it is the 'Planto de las virtudes e poesía por el magnífico señor don Iñigo López de Mendoça, Marqués de Santillana' by Jorge's cousin Gómez Manrique, and it appears, with the rest of the latter's output, in the second volume of Foulché-Delbosc's *Cancionero castellano del siglo XV*, published as volume 22 of the *Nueva Biblioteca de Autores Españoles* in 1915.[16] If Machado was a subscriber to the *Nueva Biblioteca* - and this, I think, is likely - he could have read it there in that year. This has further implications which will need to be considered presently; for the moment, it tends to confirm the date of the Don Guido poem as 1915, and hence the link with Giner.

The other obvious trace of Manrique's 'Coplas' - the metrical similarity - is, in its turn, a more ambivalent piece of evidence than might at first appear. The *pie quebrado* mixture of eight and four-syllable lines certainly defines the rhythmic character of Machado's poem, but instead of Manrique's regular alternation of two long lines and one short, we have an apparently spontaneous, irregular flow, and a somewhat greater predominance of octosyllables, with just under a quarter of the 70 lines appearing as tetrasyllables. As far as the rhyme-scheme is concerned, the repeated ABCABC of the Manriquean stanza simply does not appear here; in its place there is an indeterminate pattern, with a good many adjacent lines rhyming and - most interestingly of all - the recurrent use of an ABBA scheme - in effect, since all these instances involve octosyllabic lines, of *redondillas*. It is when we attempt to isolate these *redondilla* sections from the rest of the poem that something rather unexpected occurs. What we get is this:

> Murió don Guido, un señor
> de mozo muy jaranero
> muy galán y algo torero;
> de viejo, gran rezador.
>
> Cuando mermó su riqueza
> era su monomanía
> pensar que pensar debía
> en asentar la cabeza

y para siempre jamás...
Alguien dirá: ¿Qué dejaste?
Yo pregunto: ¿Qué llevaste
al mundo donde hoy estás?

¿Tu amor a los alamares
y a las sedas y a los oros
y a la sangre de los toros
y al humo de los altares?

That is not as good a poem as the 'Coplas por la muerte de don Guido' but it is, I think, a poem, and it is very much the kind of draft or *apunte* which might be composed as the immediate response to some actual event - the death, let us say, of some local worthy. The *redondilla* is second only to the *romance* in the facility with which it lends itself to this ironic, *noticiero* use. The opening line as it stands here suggests this still rather literal response to an anecdotal pretext; 'pensar que pensar debía...' is perhaps the characteristic bit of Machadian wit which made the lines worth jotting down at all. Once the ineptitude of Don Guido's gesture towards thinking was in focus, the questioning of its value which followed was surely consequential enough. But there are further points to be made about that questioning. It is in this version if anywhere that one can recognize that residual warmth towards the *señorito* figure which both López Estrada and Dolores Gómez Molleda have discerned; 'aún en su degradación existía una gracia'.[17] The poem in its final state takes up a harsher stance, in whose formation the contrast with Manrique's 'Coplas' plays some part. That the poem in *redondillas* ends in a question is, of course, not at all out of place, but it remains inconclusive in other senses too. It is still too obviously a little bit of anecdote and a little bit of reflection; its address to Don Guido is a mere rheme to the theme of 'Yo pregunto...'; there is not, at this stage, anyone there to ask. Nor has the anecdote yet been inserted in any wider frame of moral and social reference; it seems less clear than it needs to be who is to read it, or how. We might perhaps call it a poem that has not yet located its 'tú esencial'.[18]

If, as appears quite likely, the *redondillas* were a first draft for the poem that was eventually to become the lament for Don Guido, it was their embedding in a larger structure which gave the latter its ultimate quality. But that structure in its turn is only partly defined by the use of the Manriquean model. The rest of the poem is made up, in about equal proportions, of sections which are fairly close, if still rough-hewn, parallels to Manrique's *pie quebrado* stanzas, and of other linking material, mostly involving paired rhymes. Some of the rhyming here is broadly and consciously bathetic: *están / din-dan; asentóla / española; una / fortuna; don Guido / eres ido;* and above all, of course:

Buen don Guido y equipaje
¡buen viaje![19]

The effect is twofold. It smokes Don Guido out of his would-be refuge in a timeless, traditional rhetoric of high dignity and religious observance, and into the deflating ordinariness of a strictly contemporary language. And it prevents our taking the echoes of Manrique as implying that Don Guido ought to be more traditional in his way of life, rather than less. The grave and ancient 'Coplas' exhibit a dignity which the Andalusian *señorito* notably lacks. But Machado makes no commitment to their ideological view of Christian *caballería*. Still less is he committed to Manrique's proposition that 'cualquiera tiempo passado/fue mejor'. It is a strictly contemporary reading of the 'Coplas' which he uses to weigh and find wanting Don Guido's reading of his own role.

The four metrical episodes which most closely echo the rhythmic habit of Manrique's elegy follow the same sequence of themes as the nucleus of *redondillas*. Lines 9-14 add a rich specificity to the account of Don Guido's *mocedad*: a series of totally useless accomplishments, canonized in the admiring *qué dirán* of provincial gossip: 'Dicen que tuvo un serrallo...' Lines 23-28 give similar body to his repentance: the pompous assertion of status and antiquity; the cliché about tradition framed as Don Guido's own utterance. These quasi-stanzas approximate in all but their last two lines to Manrique's metrical dispositions, and so establish these as an implicit norm for the poem. The next such episode sharply varies that norm: lines 51-56 with their insistent *pie quebrado* hammer home abruptly the key contrast between what Don Guido can take with him and what he leaves behind:

> El acá
> y el allá,
> caballero,
> se ve en tu rostro marchito,
> lo infinito:
> cero, cero.

The Manriquean stanza is stripped of its superfluities as the Manriquean ideal is stripped of its substance by Don Guido, and he in turn is similarly exposed by death. Where the dying Rodrigo Manrique could be made the subject of a successful appeal to the poem's governing universals, for Don Guido the supreme individualist there are no universals to appeal to: he is simply a dead face on a pillow. The wit is detached, objective, almost clinical: the sign for mathematical infinity is, precisely, two noughts side by side - two closed eyes, set deep in a 'rostro marchito'. Nothing left for him in the here and now - where, for him, everything was - and not much more to be hoped for there, in the hollow spaces of the infinite. The rewriting of Manrique is at its most intense here, with the pivotal word *caballero* concentrating all the ironies in itself. By contrast, the final picture of Don Guido's lying-in-state (lines 62-67) is far closer to the Manriquean stanza-model (8/8/4 + 8/8/4), with an almost Manriquean diversity of rhymes (AABCDC). What disrupts the similarity is the impertinent (yet thematically extremely pertinent) coda: 'el caballero andaluz', bringing us down with a bump to a particular earth. The 'fin de una aristocracia', the displacement of Rodrigo Manrique's eloquent conformity with God's will into Don Guido's suspiciously pat gestures - these things are not in themselves the subject of the poem. That is very firmly established - here re-established - as an aspect of 'the way we live now', valued by the stark, unshrinking moral calculus of lines 51-56. The echoes of Manrique are a means of setting up that valuation.

There is a need for caution, even in speaking of echoes. In fact, very little of the Don Guido poem's verbal substance is derived from the older 'Coplas'. There is a sprinkling of lexical items which we might, in a general way, register as 'medieval': *diestro, doncella, blasones, tosca sayal*, and of course *caballero*. These terms supply the other component of the incongruity deliberately courted by 'din-dan', 'camino del cementerio', 'equipaje', and 'buen viaje'. They are also, in each case, subtly devalued (of the 'doncella de gran fortuna' we might perhaps say 'revalued') by the context in which they are used. The rhyme-scheme of the Don Guido poem is, with a couple of important exceptions, wholly independent of Manrique; it is not a coincidence, though, that the opening rhyme of *pulmonía / día* has the same assonance as the fifteenth-century poet's opening 'Recuerde el alma dormida', nor that Rodrigo Manrique's willing acceptance of death rhymes *ya / está*, as the crux of Machado's poem rhymes *acá / allá*. Structurally, there is a highly significant mismatch between the two poems: virtually nothing in the first twenty-four stanzas of Manrique has any parallel here at all. The Don Guido piece takes up exclusively the matter of Manrique's last two sections: the life of the man now dead, and a confrontation with the fact of death, presented in each case through direct speech.[20] This simplification of the original form is, of course, characteristic of Machado's parodic intent, and it is taken further in the treatment of each section.

Rodrigo Manrique is represented as being not just virtuous after the manner of his own estate 'tan famoso / e valiente', but virtuous in a set of worthwhile relationships:

> ... de buenos abrigo,
> amado por virtuoso
> de la gente.

He is seen as a friend to his friends, a protective overlord to his vassals and kin, an effective foe, and a mighty captain in war. We might doubt the value of some of these. (Machado in 1915 was certainly having his doubts about the last of them.[21]) We might, with much justice, doubt whether the real Rodrigo Manrique was all that he was claimed to be. But at least he was something and for somebody; what and for whom was Don Guido? It is not only the recorded trivialities in Machado's portrait of him which give the reply ('un maestro / en refrescar manzanilla'): it is that portrait's devastating silences. The Count of Paredes is confronted at the last by an allegorized Death, who addresses him with respect as 'Buen caballero...' This Death sets out the hierarchical contrast between the life of this 'mundo engañoso', the life of fame which will outlast it, and the eternity into which Rodrigo must now depart; the latter, equal to the challenge, makes his Christian end. But Don Guido is apostrophized after the event, by the sceptical voice of his narrator: 'Buen don Guido...' and 'caballero' are no longer unambiguously honorific. Don Guido has left not even fame behind; he makes no claim in his own person, and indeed can lay claim to nothing beyond the hollow *formalidad* in which he has lived and died.[22] Again, the Manrique poem is made simultaneously present and absent. Large parts of it, as we have seen, are absent altogether: the whole of its defining allegory of life as river and road, which meant so much to Machado elsewhere; the whole of the *Ubi sunt* passage which Juan de Mairena was to expound as exemplary. These things, being absent, become a kind of measure of how far short Don Guido falls of the seriousness either of dying or of being dead.[23]

There is, perhaps, a similar resonance in the other allusion made by Machado's title. There seem at first glance to be no matters of substance in which the Don Guido poem recalls Gómez Manrique's 'Planto de las virtudes'. It is not, like that work, a lament uttered by the Virtues; nor is it even in any specific fashion a commemoration of virtues Don Guido had, or might have thought he had. What may well be more significant, on the other hand, is the fact that Gómez Manrique was commemorating the Marqués de Santillana, the supreme example in his day of a *caballero sabio*, eminent alike in arms and letters. The contrasting void presented by the mediocre Don Guido, the *caballero necio*, the *gran señor* reduced to *señorito* proportions, could be left to tell its own tale.

This habit of making poetry out of absences and silences is widespread in Machado; it might well seem especially important in terms of some of his later philosophical speculations. It was, in any case, a valuable approach for the exercise in which he was engaged in bringing the Manriquean 'Coplas' to bear upon Don Guido. That exercise can very well be described in terms like 'de-coding' and 'de-creation' - precisely the language which Beth Miller applies to Lázara Meldiú. Indeed, in the sequence of the three *caballeros*, the real work of de-coding seems to have gone on, not between the male poet Antonio Machado and the feminist Meldiú, but between Manrique and Machado. But in that case, how autonomous can Meldiú's reading of Machado be? In particular, does her poem open up a set of relations which discloses itself only to an awareness of her as a woman writer, in a circumstance substantially defined by men? That or something like it, presumably, is what a feminist critical approach would want to assert.

The assertion can be upheld, I believe; moreover, it can be done without impugning Machado's capacity to address Meldiú as reader in terms of his own agenda, rather than of hers. But to get to that point, we shall need to follow another route than the simple opposition of 'this woman poet' to 'male poets'. We might more usefully begin with some of the contrasts between 'Don Guido' and 'Caballero'. Machado does, to an extent, assume an overtly oppositional stance within an existing tradition. These are *coplas*, but they travesty Manrique's 'Coplas', as Don Guido travesties his own pretensions to traditional grandeur and devotion. Meldiú, by contrast, subverts - so far as poetic tradition is concerned - only the modestly-scaled lyric model which she herself has adopted. It is hardly, as it stands, a contrast between masculine and feminine strategies. Some readers, it is true, might be more surprised if the terms of the contrast were reversed. But Meldiú was not prevented by her gender from undertaking parody on a large scale, or Machado by his from delicate, localized subversion. To call Machado's rhetoric of absences and non-affirmations a 'feminine' element in his poetic range would again be gratuitous. But there would be nothing gratuitous about suggesting that for such a woman reader as Lázara Meldiú, who on the evidence of this poem clearly found the unanalysed assertion of *caballero* values by male poets tiresome, this mode of writing would have carried some special interest.

There is a contrast again in the way in which the central figure in each poem is envisaged and confronted. Don Guido has a name, and a local habitation that goes with it ('este señor de Sevilla'; 'el caballero andaluz'). He also has a very definite biography; though evanescent in the actual moment of the poem, this is what the entire first half of the Machado piece is all about. Little of this *equipaje*, however, is likely to survive the encounter with death. Indeed, all of that is already memory: we catch our glimpse of Don Guido himself as he is on his way, definitively, *out*. Lázara Meldiú takes issue with a much more anonymous and emblematic figure, named only in her title (and without so much as a definite or indefinite article at that). This *caballero* has no personal history that we can discern, though he is heavy with History. He is, above all else, a cultural presence - or to be more accurate still, a cultural *quantity*. We might, with fair justice, say that Don Guido is imagined with some realism - an Aristotelian, mimetic creation, known to the understanding because known to the senses. Meldiú's *caballero* is Platonic, abstract, archetypal, the product of a poetry which sees its business as having to do with loftier matters than the experiential. And that, surely, must point us away from the facile trap of seeing the concrete representation as 'male' art and the abstract, generalized one as 'female'. The abstract idiom of 'Caballero' is, quite simply, what Spanish-Americans in the first few decades of this century tended to believe poems should be like. Men or women, unless they had well-developed alternative views, they were liable to write at that level of generality.

And yet Meldiú's poem does have a specifically local dimension - if for 'local' we can accept a meaning as broad as 'Spanish-American'. No longer tied to Seville, her *caballero* is very clearly bound up with the Peninsula, with the institutions of Church and State which were brought over from there, and with the processes - relevantly, they are processes of conquest - by which they got to the New World. *Raza*, as Miller points out, is a pertinent term in this; so is *pirata*. And there is weight in the general contention that social class, *criollo* racial priority, male presumption, religious and regalist ideologies, and even the 'rancia lírica' of outmoded literary conventions are here subsumed in a single imposition. If Lázara Meldiú has found it natural to represent that imposition in somewhat abstracted form, the response to it which she offers - as a Mexican, as a *poetisa*, as the 'Indianist' who was to produce *Nacu-Xanat*, and as a woman - is no less rooted in historical circumstance than is the more tangibly detailed rebuttal of Don Guido's way of being which Antonio Machado puts forward.

Nor is there much to choose between the two in point of commitment - indeed, of hostility towards their respective protagonists. The human type abstracted by 'Caballero' (though frequently passing himself off as such) is no good news to women. Don Guido and his like were little better news to Andalusian country schoolmasters like Machado, to local Sevillan intellectuals like his father and grandfather, to the Giners of Ronda, and the de los Ríos, to poets generally. When García Lorca called his *granadino* fellow-citizens 'la peor burguesía de España' he was claiming for them a position for which there was keen local competition.[24] Behind the tactical ironies and controlled voice of the 'Coplas por la muerte de don Guido' there is a whole pressure of liberal humanist indignation against the intolerable falsehoods and oppressions of Don Guido's world. It would be wholly misplaced to found a male-against-feminist contrast between these two poems on the claim that Meldiú was irreconcilably subversive of her *caballero*, and Machado ultimately complicit in Don Guido's (or even, for different reasons, Rodrigo Manrique's) version of patriarchy.

Yet there is a palpable difference in the ways which these two poets find of managing their own antipathy to the subjects they address. If Machado's original *redondilla* draft (assuming that to have existed) was a little gentler than his eventual poem, that might well be because a certain inhibition tempered his critical assessment of an individual, however worthless, who was only recently dead. Such a self-limitation would be very like Antonio Machado. Yet there is no denying that the Don Guido verses in their final form do embrace a certain geniality of tone. This element, however, is not addressed to Don Guido. Like much of the poem itself, it is directed past him, at Machado's target-audience - the audience which will respond to the note of relief implicit in 'Al fin una pulmonía / mató a Don Guido...' That conversational opening, its shared assumptions quickly made explicit in what follows, invokes a kind of 'society of the poem'. The reader is drawn into a fellowship with 'Palacio buen amigo...', with the pupils of Giner, with Unamuno the recipient of Machado's letters about life in Baeza. We are made, one might say, into honorary members of the Generation of 1898 - and that, after all, was what the best of that generation at their best sought to do for their compatriots. When Rodrigo Alvarez Molina writes that Antonio Machado 'no se dirige a una minoría determinada, sino que canta para toda la sociedad española, aunque se piense más en la clase intelectual', he is putting in a static way something which, in poems like this, is a matter of dynamics and intentionality.[25] One of the reasons why Machado does in fact make his poetry so widely communicable is that he wanted it to be so. Here even the lines addressed to Don Guido himself (from whom, of course, no response is to be expected) are locked into that larger address to those who understand and to those who can be brought to understand. There is a rich mixture of effects from the blatant ('buen viaje...') to the enigmatic ('lo infinito / cero, cero'), from the palpably physical ('los párpados de cera,/ y la fina calavera') to the abstract and conceptual ('¡tan formal!'). By being readily party to some, the reader is drawn into being party to others. By contrast with the putative fragment in *redondillas*, the poem has found its 'tú esencial'. But it is not the person therein addressed as *tú*.

That at least Machado has in common with Lázara Meldiú, but for wholly different reasons - reasons which at last do seem to connect with a specifically feminist concern. By contrast with Machado, she is not pronouncing the last word on an individual who - however obstinately the social forces which he represents may persist - is himself at long last dead. She is addressing the incarnation of forces which leave her, in a multiplicity of ways, isolated and vulnerable - so much so that her first three stanzas do not even find her a place in her own poem. The dominant, invading *tú* is omnipresent. The fourth stanza, with its extravagant 'trino de alondras', asserts her selfhood very dramatically - and on that specificially female ground where she is most isolated and most vulnerable. Through that ordering of her material she is able to speak, as it were, around the edges of her poem, addressing those who will recognize the threatening and inherently unjust aspects of her cultural circumstance (stanzas 1-3) and the integrity of her counter-attack - again an implied reader very different from the *tú* formally addressed. All this we can well acknowledge as a feminist strategy, made desirable for her by that woman's situation to which the account of the *caballero* bears contrastive witness. Yet this feminist strategy was not made inescapable by gender as such; obviously there were other kinds of poem which she might have written, but did not. The strategy, well-chosen as it turned out to be, was a matter of her choice. It seems clear that what Antonio Machado did before her in 'Don Guido' - including what he did as a reader unmaking and remaking Manrique's 'Coplas' - tangibly facilitated that choice. Hers, in its turn, is a re-creation, not a decreation of Machado. That, arguably, is what he is able to reach towards from any reader; it is in so doing that he achieves his particular availability for so many of them. And not least, surely, for a woman reader. With some sense of inevitability one recalls the first recorded production of the *máquina de trovar*:

> Dicen que el hombre no es hombre
> mientras que no oye su nombre
> de labios de una mujer.
> Puede ser.[26]

NOTES

1   See Aurora de Albornoz, 'Bibliografía de Antonio Machado' in *Homenaje a Antonio Machado, La Torre*, 45-46 (1964), 505-53.

2   Ricardo Gullón, *Una poética para Antonio Machado* (Madrid: Gredos, 1970), p. 264; cf. Rubén Darío, 'Antonio Machado' in *Obras poéticas completas* (Buenos Aires: 'El Ateneo', 1953), p. 783.

3   Manuel Tuñón de Lara, *Antonio Machado, poeta del pueblo* (Barcelona: Laia, 1975; 1st edn., 1967), p. 287.

4   Beth Miller, ed., *Women in Hispanic Literature: Icons and Fallen Idols* (Berkeley: California UP, 1983), pp. 18-19

5   See José Luis Martínez, *Literatura mexicana siglo XX, 1910-1949* (Mexico: Robredo, 1949-50); Gabriel Zaid, *Omnibús de poesía mexicana* (Mexico: Siglo XXI, 1972); B. Costa Amic, *Cien poetas mexicanos* (Mexico: Libro Mex, 1957); Salvador Novo, *Mil y un sonetos mexicanos del siglo XVI al XX* (Mexico: Porrúa, 1963).

6   Natalia Gamiz, *Mujeres de América: antología* (Mexico: Continental, 1946), pp. 308-10; Etelvina Villanueva y Saavedra, *Ronda femenina de América: poesías* (La Paz: Fenix, 1953), pp. 365-66. Contrast Carmen Conde: *Once grandes poetisas americohispanas* (Madrid: Cultura Hispánica, 1967).

7   Concha Espina, *De Antonio Machado a su grande y secreto amor* (Madrid: Gráficas Reunidas, 1950); Dora Isella Russell, 'De Antonio Machado. Poesías de guerra', *El País* (Montevideo), 13 May 1962.

8   Villanueva y Saavedra, pp. 365-66; Gamiz, p. 310.

9   See Nicholas G. Round, 'Formal Integration in Jorge Manrique's "Coplas por la muerte de su padre"' in *Readings in Spanish and Portuguese Poetry for Geoffrey Connell*, ed. N.G. Round and D. Gareth Walters (Glasgow University Department of Hispanic Studies, 1985), p. 205; Julio Rodríguez Puértolas, 'Jorge Manrique y la manipulación de la historia' in *Medieval and Renaissance Studies in Honour of Robert Brian Tate*, ed. Ian Michael and Richard A. Cardwell (Oxford: Dolphin, 1986), pp. 123-33.

10   Other instances are cited by Rodrigo Alvarez Molina, *Variaciones sobre Antonio Machado: el hombre y su lenguaje* (Madrid: Insula, 1973), p. 39.

11   Francisco López Estrada, 'Antonio Machado y Sevilla' in *Curso en Homenaje a Antonio Machado* (Salamanca: Universidad, 1975), p. 157.

12   Letter of 1913 (undated) in *Poesía y prosa*, III, p. 1534.

13   Aurora de Albornoz, *La presencia de Miguel de Unamuno en Antonio Machado* (Madrid: Gredos, 1968), p. 199; cf. also pp. 196-98, citing Unamuno's essays 'Sobre Don Juan Tenorio' (1908) and 'Ibsen y Kierkegaard' (1907).

14   Helen F. Grant, '"Angulos de enfoque" en la poesía de Antonio Machado', *La Torre*, 45-46, 472-73; also Tuñón de Lara, p. 123. Cf. the text of the Giner poem in *PP*, 587-88.

15   Text of the 'Coplas' in Jorge Manrique, *Obras* ed. Antonio Serrano de Haro (Madrid: Alhambra, 1976), pp. 241-300.

16   *Cancionero castellano del siglo XV*, ed. R. Foulché-Delbosc, II (Madrid: Bailly-Baillière. 1915), 66-85.

17   López Estrada, p. 160; also Dolores Gómez Molleda, 'Algunos aspectos del pensamiento de Antonio Machado en el marco ideológico y social de su tiempo' in *Curso en homenaje a Antonio Machado*, p. 88.

18   Cf. 'Proverbios y cantares': 'No es el yo fundamental / eso que busca el poeta,/ sino el tú esencial.' (*PP*, 633). See also Alvarez Molina, p. 20, citing 'Problemas de la lírica' (1917): 'El sentimiento no es una creación del sujeto individual... Hay siempre en él una colaboración del TU, es decir, de otros sujetos.'

19   Antonio Sánchez Barbudo (*Los poemas de Antonio Machado. Los temas. El sentimiento y la expresión* (Barcelona: Lumen, 1967), p. 299) shrewdly defines this tone: 'la elegía, más que a don Jorge Manrique, recuerda a veces populares aleluyas en papeles de colores.'

20   On the internal structure of Manrique's 'Coplas' see Round, pp. 205-21, especially pp. 206, 219 for the alternative views of Navarro Tomás, Gilman, Aguirre, Salinas, and Orduna.

21   See his letter to Unamuno of 31 December 1914 in *Poesía y prosa*, III, p. 1558: 'Yo empiezo a dudar de la santidad del patriotismo.'

22   On the 'hollowness' of such figures cf. Grant, p. 471.

23   Cf. Gullón p. 191 on the 'double distancing' achieved in this poem: 'la visible y constatable entre *autor y figura*' and 'la invisible y sutil entre *figura y arquetipo*'. The latter 'convierte a la figura en contrafigura y... hace más vasta la profundidad del poema'.

24   Ian Gibson, *The Death of Lorca* (London: W.H. Allen, 1973), p. 43; see also the comments of Giner de los Ríos on the shallowness of conventional religiosity, quoted by Gómez Molleda, p. 59; ibid., p. 55 on Machado's family background.

25   Alvarez Molina, p. 24.

26   'Diálogo entre *Juan de Mairena y Jorge Meneses*' (*PP*, 713).

Nuevas canciones (1917-1920). Machado, the *avant-garde* and the *neopopularismo* of the 1927 Generation

DEREK GAGEN

University College, Swansea

Between 1917 and 1923 Spain experienced a social and political crisis of great magnitude. Following the Renovación movement of 1917 the Restoration system was in disarray and the folly of the Africanist fling in Morocco was increasingly plain to see. Yet this is a peculiarly rich time for Spanish poetry. The late nineteen-tens and early twenties see the great landmark of Jiménez's *Segunda antolojía poética* of 1922, the *avant-garde* breakthrough with *ultra* and Huidobro's *creacionismo*, the early poetic works of Lorca, Diego, Alonso, Salinas and Chabás, followed in 1925 by Alberti's *Marinero en tierra*. The three key words of the period are: *lo puro*, epitomized in Juan Ramón's first summa, the *Segunda antolojía*; *lo neuvo*, the desire to go *ultra*, to 'Repudiar lo trillado/para ganar lo otro', as Diego put it in the opening poem of *Imagen*;[1] and *lo popular*, the *neopopularismo* epitomized by the *cante jondo* festival organized by Lorca in Granada in 1922 and by his and Alberti's early verse. The literary world was bubbling with excitement - a diversion perhaps from *El chirrión de los políticos*, as Azorín entitled his vituperative *fantasía* of 1923 - with short-lived little magazines or grander periodicals publishing new work from young and old alike.

Antonio Machado was by now very much an established figure within the literary world. His name appears in several of these publications: *Índice, Horizonte, Alfar* and, of course, *Los Lunes del Imparcial* and *España*. Moreover, in 1924 he published a new book of verse, *Nuevas canciones (1917-1920)*. For the *ultraístas*, intent upon moving Spanish verse on from the *novecentismo* that they regarded as dead, a new work by Machado might be viewed as old hat. But by 1924 the literary world was, like the political world, changing. Writing in his autobiography of his decision to include in *Marinero en tierra* the more formalist poems such as the *sonetos alejandrinos* or the opening poem 'Sueño del marinero', Alberti commented:

> ¿Era yo un desertor de la poesía hasta entonces llamada de vanguardia por volver al cultivo de ciertas formas conocidas? No. La nueva y verdadera vanguardia íbamos a ser nosotros... Aquella otra vanguardia primera, la ultraísta, estaba en retirada.[2]

100

Of course the *ultraístas* were not going to avoid challenging such a development. Reviewing Diego's *Soria* in the first number of *Revista de Occidente*, Antonio Espina emphasized its traditionalism that was so notably different from the tone of *Imagen* but insisted that 'la suerte está echada. Hay que marchar hacia adelante'.[3] A question was being posed. *Lo puro* and *lo nuevo* were acceptable. Were *lo popular* and *lo tradicional?*

Machado's choice of title for the 1924 collection seems to make his own stance quite clear. *Nuevas canciones* as a title asserts the continuing tradition of the folksong, *lo nuevo* in the sense of a renewal or reinterpretation of the lyric tradition.

Some of the reviewers of *Nuevas canciones* found this puzzling. Díez-Canedo led later commentators into a critical cul-de-sac by writing about hai-kus.[4] *Revista de Occidente* asked Eugenio Montes to review the book. This was a significant choice for Montes was identified with the *esprit nouveau* in literary Madrid. (He was the 'mi Virgilio' to whom Diego dedicated the poem 'Creacionismo' that marks the turning point from *ultraísmo* to *creacionismo* in *Imagen*.) To Montes the title *Nuevas canciones* seemed slightly inexact:

> Ciertamente, hay en el libro que glosamos, nuevas canciones, pero hay nuevas definiciones, igualmente. No siempre la voz de Machado se desata en olas musicales, como la vena pinchada por la aguja. En ocasiones se recorta en llanos decires, pronunciados sin altos ni bajos, indiferentes a la línea melódica; en sentencias y evaluaciones sobrias y lacónicas, de carácter más bien especulativo, que resumen, más la apasionada experiencia personal, una tranquila y aprendida milenaria experiencia colectiva.[5]

Montes sums up the work rather more accurately here than most later commentators. The songs are different from the laconic, sententious *proverbios y cantares*. He went on to note how many of the later poems were *pièces de circonstance* and that this perhaps conflicted with the golden rule of *ultra*: 'nada de anecdótico'.[6] Montes finished by noting the scarcity of imagery, a marked contrast of course with that *avant-garde* fashion that cherished the 'higher algebra of metaphor'. Yet we note that, despite the charge of anecdote and paucity of imagery, Montes found in *Nuevas canciones* elements in tune with at least one contemporary lyric mode, namely the use of traditional verse, *neopopularismo*.

This is worth noting since at times we receive an inaccurate impression of Machado's relationship to the young poets of the 1927 Generation. Perhaps Castellet must shoulder some of the blame. Despite his disclaimer that he is referring only to Machado's poetics as conveyed in the draft Academy speech, in *Un cuarto de siglo de poesía española* the Catalan critic actually cites texts from as early as 1916 and 1924 to plot Machado's attack on symbolism and his vision of *objetividad* and *fraternidad*.[7] Quoting Cernuda's dictum that 'el poeta se había acabado antes que el escritor', he perceives 'un concepto temporal y realista de la poesía' in the later work (59). Even the finely judged chapter in Donald Shaw's *The Generation of 1989 in Spain* (London: Benn, 1975) concentrates on the reflective verse in *Nuevas canciones* as well as on the sonnets of 'Glosando a Ronsard' and 'Los sueños dialogados', which incidentally come from the section entitled 'Folklore' in the 1924 text.

It seems likely, then, that our awareness of Machado's later development may be tempting critics to neglect elements within *Nuevas canciones* that are encompassed in that area of *lo popular* that Alberti and others saw as the true *avant-garde*. Such a perception is supported if we consult the review by Cansinos-Asséns in *El Imparcial*. Cansinos is a particularly useful witness. Despite his fame as virtually the elaborator of *ultraísmo* he was also the most consistently acute writer on the traditional lyric among the regular literary reviewers of the time. Not surprisingly Cansinos highlighted the significance of the adjective in Machado's title:

> en el título del libro de Machado el adjetivo tiene únicamente un sentido cronológico, no tratándose de ningún nuevo evangelio de arte, sino de las últimas canciones que han brotado de sus labios.

And yet, Cansinos adds, it is an indication of the times that this poet who usually delights in evocations of the past 'haya cedido también a la atracción de lo nuevo, tan poderosa hoy'.[8] However surprising this may seem to those who rely for their view of Machado's development on the rewriting of literary history by Castellet and others, it seems clear that Machado was only slowly evolving towards the views expressed in *Reflexiones sobre la lírica* and the *Proyecto de un discurso de ingreso en la Academia de la Lengua*. As yet his anathemas were directed towards the *ultra*-Huidobro-Guillén wing rather than the *neopopularista* tendency in the 1927 group of poets.

There is an abundance of evidence that Machado was sensitive to the development of Spanish lyric at this time. He advised the young Rafael Laínez in Baeza to lay aside his Darío and gave him instead Juan Ramón's *Diario de un poeta reciéncasado*, 'el último libro de un gran poeta, de un verdadero poeta'.[9] As is well known, he was visited by the young Lorca in June 1916 and the following year.[10] By that time Machado had already written the note on Huidobro that appears in *Los complementarios*. After his move to Segovia he was visited by a group of young poets, including Salinas; 'En tren' from *Nuevas canciones* is dedicated 'A los jóvenes poetas que me honraron con su visita en Segovia' (*PP*, 656).[11] *Los complementarios* includes poems by Juan Ramón, Pérez de Ayala, Moreno Villa, Salinas, Ardavín and Diego as well as Valéry and Blok. Machado's concern for the new generation of poets in the early twenties is perhaps best illustrated by the cases of Diego and Alberti. Machado wrote to Diego on 4 October 1920 thanking him for a copy of *El romancero de la novia* and doubting whether 'en sus nuevos moldes creacionistas haga usted nada tan puro, tan claro, de una emoción tan clara'. The letter shows Machado to be an attentive reader of the *ultraísta* magazine *Grecia* which, once cured of 'bizantismo y chochez parisina, sería admirable'. It was 'lo más interesante que hoy se publica en España' (*Poesía y prosa*, III, pp. 1617-18). Here there is no lofty disdain for the new lyric. Indeed Machado followed Diego's progress and published brief articles on him in *La Voz de Soria*, in September 1922, one being a review of *Imagen* (*Poesía y prosa*, III, pp. 1640-41).[12] In the latter Diego's book is described as 'el primer fruto logrado de la novísima lírica española'. To be sure Machado notes the 'marcada tendencia hacia la objetividad lírica' yet this seems to be not so much the process described by Castellet as that device of linking differing planes of reality to create a new reality analysed by Debicki in his study of Diego's imagery.[13] More significantly, after the frequently quoted statement that 'la lírica estaba enferma de subjetividad', Machado discusses the theory of multiple imagery put into practice by Diego in the second section of *Imagen*, notes the role of images as means and not as ends in themselves, and particularly emphasizes the poems of section three of *Imagen*, entitled 'Estribillo':

> Mas en el libro de Gerardo Diego, donde acaso sobran imágenes, no falta emoción, alma, energía poética. Hay, además, verdaderos prodigios de técnica y en algunas composiciones, una sana nostalgia de elementalidad lírica, de retorno a la inspiración popular (*Poesía y prosa*, III, p. 1641).

Imagen, as has already been noted, consists of three sections: 'Evasión', the *ultraísta* section; 'Imagen múltiple', the *creacionista* section which contains 'Angelus', dedicated to Machado; and 'Estribillo', the more musical section that starts with a song-like poem dedicated to Falla and ends with the 'Epigramas' reminiscent at once of Machado's more sentencious *coplas* and of Gómez de la Serna's more bizarre *greguerías*. The fact is that a book such as *Imagen* was as much an admixture of new and traditional elements as was *Nuevas canciones*. Ironically, Machado anticipated Espina's later judgment on Diego's *Soria*:

> Estas dos notas, aparentemente contradictorias, son señales inequívocas del trabajo de tanteo y exploración del joven poeta (*Poesía y prosa*, III, p. 1641).

When Machado was on the jury for the Premio Nacional de Literatura for 1924-25 two books of verse were prizewinners, one of them being Diego's *Versos humanos*, a collection of sonnets, glosses, *canciones*, *elegías* and other traditional forms, cast in his *poesía relativa* mould. Yet in Machado's personal anthology of 'Poetas españoles' in *Los complementarios*, Diego was represented by a pair of poems from *Imagen*, 'Nocturno funambulesco' and 'Fe' from the 'Evasión' and 'Imagen múltiple' sections respectively. He did not choose to copy any lyric from the more traditional verse of the 'Estribillo' section, presumably because, as he noted in the *cuaderno*, 'Gerardo Diego ha encontrado el título y emplea el tono que mejor cuadra a la nueva poesía' (*Poesía y prosa*, III, p. 1223).

The other prize-winner that year was Alberti's *Marinero en tierra*, and Machado's relationship with that poet confirms the picture of a figure firmly in touch with the literary world of the nineteen-twenties and in sympathy at least with those poets who were technically assured and, preferably, in tune with the folk tradition. This contrasts with the position at the end of the decade when, in response to the *Gaceta Literaria* questionnaire '¿Cómo veo la nueva juventud española?', Machado included both Diego and Alberti among those allegedly 'contaminados del barroco francés - cartesianismo rezagado -' (*Poesía y prosa*, III, p. 1764).

Alberti's first published poems appeared in *Horizonte* in 1922 alongside Lorca's 'Baladilla de los tres ríos' and some *canciones* of Machado. As Alberti recalls in his autobiography:

> Aquel nuevo *Horizonte* sabía responder a su título. En su amplia línea despejada volvieron a hermanarse poetas momentánea y deliberadamente excluidos por 'Ultra'. Al lado de Machado ya otra vez se encontraba Juan Ramón. Del primitivo barco vanguardista, muy pocos de sus tripulantes habían logrado hacer brazo hasta la playa.[14]

It made good sense for Garfias's new magazine to include Alberti alongside Machado, whose verse had been recited by Alberti and his sister Pepita when they were teenagers.[15] When Claudio de la Torre suggested to Alberti that he present his manuscript of what was to become *Marinero en tierra* for the National Literary Prize, revealing that the jury included Machado, Menéndez Pidal, Miró, Arniches, Gabriel Maura and Moreno Villa, the young poet thought it a joke.[16] From the autobiographies of Moreno Villa and Alberti we know that the jury was divided and that the decision to award a prize to Alberti was influenced by the advocacy of Moreno Villa and Machado. Machado left a slip of paper in the typescript that was returned to Alberti:

Mar y tierra
Rafael Alberti
Es a mi juicio el mejor libro de poemas presentado al concurso.
Antonio Machado[17]

Machado had found in *Imagen*, when he reviewed it in 1922, 'emoción, alma, energía poética' (*Poesía y prosa*, III, p. 1641). We may judge that the poet of *Nuevas canciones* would have found in *Marinero en tierra* those same qualities. More significantly, however, *Marinero en tierra* marks together with Lorca's early books of verse the highpoint of the neopopularist movement. This was the area in which Machado recognizably stood alongside the young poets. As Alberti was to note:

> Antonio Machado no amaba lo barroco, contra el cual arremete por boca de su Juan de Mairena. Era el anti-Góngora, aunque él reconociera la genialidad del poeta cordobés...
>
> Y como andaluz, niño de infancia por jardines y patios del Palacio de las Dueñas de Sevilla, había bebido en el cántaro fresco de la copla popular, de la pasión directa, sin adorno, de la sentencia sabia, sin disfraces, subida escuetamente de la garganta honda de su pueblo.[18]

Alberti's emphasis on the content of popular tradition here is significant. After all, we might expect the author of *Marinero en tierra* to find a kindred spirit in Machado, perhaps for example to light upon the series 'Hacia tierra baja' from *Nuevas canciones*. Some of these lyrics would readily have found a home in the second part of *Marinero en tierra* in 1925:

> Una noche de verano.
> El tren hacia el puerto va,
> devorando aire marino.
> Aún no se ve la mar. (*PP*, 611)

with its obvious reference to Alberti's native Puerto de Santa María, the home of Machado's brother Francisco, and its use of the feminine definite article for *mar*; or poem V of the series 'Una noche de verano,/en la playa de Sanlúcar' (*PP*, 612), reminiscent of the later copla of Machado 'Desde Sevilla a Sanlúcar', which John Cummins cites as an example of Machado's usage of traditional content and wording.[19] In 1925 Juan Ramón described Machado as 'perpetuo marinero en tierra eterna'.[20] The identification with the young neopopularists was clear, for the *topoi* of *poesía de tipo tradicional* abound in *Nuevas canciones* rendering it quite characteristic of Spanish poetry around 1924.[21]

Why, then, has this not been recongized by later commentators? Almost certainly because of the point that Alberti hinted at in the passage from *Imagen primera de...* quoted above, namely that Machado's *popularismo* was *Folklore*, increasingly a matter of content rather than the formal conventions of traditional verse (parallelism, the *cancionero* vocative, etc.), and because the critical eye has been caught by reminiscences of the earlier Machado. *Nuevas canciones*, in short, has to some extent been judged by the yardstick of what Machado had been and what he was to become. To develop Juan Ramón's perceptive characterization, Alberti was a 'marinero en tierra' but Machado was the 'perpetuo marinero en tierra eterna'.

For most critics from Salinas in 1933, to Pradal Rodríguez (1949), Valverde (1971) and Sesé (1975), *Nuevas canciones* is characterized by its diversity.[22] Setting the work in the context of the poetry published in those years Sesé alludes to the 'inspiración nueva, como un soplo de frescor, de gracia ingenua y popular' in the early works of Diego, Alonso, Salinas and Alberti whereas

> De manera más general, en Antonio Machado el tono es más grave, más austero, más sentencioso que en todos estos últimos poetas, en quienes brilla la juventud.[23]

While we might wish to argue that the underlying message of Diego and Alberti is possibly more austere than Sesé suggested, we can agree with his general observation. Machado's graver and more sententious lyric accorded well with what were hardly the banquet years for most Spaniards. Such a tone certainly conveyed accurately his sense of *lo popular* and *folklore* in the years when he was writing the verse collected in the 1924 edition of *Nuevas canciones*. This may also help us to appreciate how the diverse content of *Nuevas canciones* corresponds to Machado's understanding of the term *folklore*.

The dates of *Nuevas canciones* were given by Machado in the 1924 edition as '1917-1920', a period of civil dissension and literary debate in which it is easy enough to establish the poet's frame of mind.[24] Obviously, in the literary sphere his concern was with the emerging rhetoric of *Ultra* and the *novísimos*. The two sections 'Sobre el empleo de las imágenes en el arte' and 'Sobre las imágenes en la lírica' from *Los complementarios* seem to arise from Machado's reading of Vicente Huidobro's *Horizon Carré* (1917) and *Ecuatorial* (1918).[25] In *Horizon Carré* Huidobro proposed to:

> Créer un poème en empruntant à la vie ses motifs et en les transformant pour leur donner une vie nouvelle et indépendante.
> Rien d'anecdotique ni de descriptif. L'émotion doit naître de la seule vertu créatrice.
> Faire un POEME comme la nature fait un arbre.[26]

To Machado this view of the lyric process was clearly unacceptable. Art was losing the sense of its own importance. For lyric poetry this was particularly dangerous:

> Cuando el poeta duda de que el centro del universo está en su propio corazón, de que su espíritu es fuente que mana, foco que irradia energía creadora capaz de informar y aun de deformar el mundo en torno; entonces el espíritu del poeta vaga desconcertado nuevamente en torno a los objetos (*Poesía y prosa*, III, p. 1214).

For Machado the fetishism of objects was symptomatic of a deep crisis: lyric poetry, at a critical time in human history, was off target. Yet he does not dismiss the entire poetics of *ultraísmo* and *creacionismo*. Referring to 'Los cantos de los niños' he claims to have

106

anticipated the 'estética novísima' in proclaiming 'el derecho de la lírica a *contar* la pura emoción, borrando la totalidad de la historia humana'. None the less, he adds, 'la coincidencia de mi propósito de entonces no iba más allá de esta abolición de lo anecdótico' (*Poesía y prosa*, III, 1207). The key lines from 'Los cantos de los niños convey this succinctly:

> confusa la historia
> y clara la pena ...   (*PP*, 434)

This poem is seen by Valverde as holding the keys, 'temporalidad y comunidad', to Machado's poetics.[27] It is certainly clear that the poetic intention is closer, let us say, to the Lorca of the lectures on *Cante jondo* and *Las nanas infantiles* than to the aesthetics of Huidobro's 'Tour Eiffel':

> Tour Eiffel
> Guitarre du ciel.
> > Ta télégraphie sans fil
> > Attire les mots
> > Comme un rosier les abeilles.[28]

This is in Diego's terms 'absolute' imagery: in Machado's 'objective' imagery. (It may be noted that Machado failed to discern the element of popular or traditional inspiration in some of the apparently *avant-garde* poems, such as 'Guitarra' from Juan Chabás's *Espejos* of 1921.) In general the new poets sought in Borges's phrase 'una visión inédita de algún fragmento de la vida' and metaphor thus became the chief object of lyric poetry.[29] For Machado 'sólo un espíritu trivial, una inteligencia limitada al radio de la sensación, puede recrearse enturbiando conceptos con metáforas' (*Poesía y prosa*, III, p. 1209). The true purpose of verse was to convey the *pena* that was as discernible in the children's songs as in the waters of the fountain:

> Yo escucho los cantos
> de viejas cadencias,
> que los niños cantan
> cuando en coro juegan,
> y vierten en coro
> sus almas que sueñan,
> cual vierten sus aguas
> las fuentes de piedra...   (*PP*, 433)

It is surely significant that Machado recalled this poem when grappling with the issues raised by the new poetics for the 'clara... pena' derived essentially from Machado's understanding of the process of poetic tradition, to which his contribution was *Nuevas canciones*. This book, in other words, is a significant step in his response to the challenge of *creacionismo* and *L'esprit nouveau*.

Of course, as Alberti pointed out, Machado's interest in traditional verse had always been well known. However, it clearly came to the fore in the late 1910s. Reading the prologues written in 1917 and 1919 we are struck by the references to tradition. In the prologue to *Campos de Castilla*, his mission is seen as 'inventar nuevos poemas de lo eterno humano' (*Poesía y prosa*, III, p. 1594), a foretaste of the *auto-folklore* of *Nuevas canciones*. The importance of invention is emphasized. Machado was fleeing from the grotesque pastiches of ballad and folksong that were widely seen as 'poesía popular'. His concern in the ballads was with 'lo elemental humano'. Yet clearly, as we have seen from his reaction to Huidobro's *creacionista* works, Machado was also profoundly aware of the contemporary social and political crises. The prologue to the second edition of *Soledades, galerías, otros poemas*, dated April 1919, makes this clear in the well-known passage in which Machado spoke of his love of 'la edad que se avecina' and of 'los poetas que han de surgir, cuando una tarea común apasione las almas' (*Poesía y prosa*, III, p. 1603). It was his fear that the *avant-garde* might diminish the role of poetry socially that would make Machado express dismay at the image-laden Baroque intricacies of *Ultra* and, later, the Góngora tercentenary. But the old style folklorist in Machado saw an eternal message, as clear as the grief enshrined in the children's playground songs. 'Sólo lo eterno, lo que nunca dejó de ser, será otra vez revelado, y la fuente homérica volverá a fluir' (*Poesía y prosa*, III, p. 1603).

Machado, then, was opposing *lo eterno* to *lo nuevo* and he refers here for the first time to the myth of Demeter, which was to be deployed in 'Olivo del camino' in *Indice* (1922) and in the fuller version that opens *Nuevas canciones*:

> Deméter, de la hoz de oro, tomará en sus brazos - como el día antiguo al hijo de Keleos - al vástago tardío de la agotada burguesía y, tras criarle a sus pechos, le envolverá otra vez en la llama divina. (*Poesía y prosa*, III, pp. 1603-04).

The poem itself has been heavily criticized but the significant point for the present discussion is that the sense of a positive future for the *pueblo* accords with Machado's sense of a progressive message within traditional lyric. This is *folklore* of a type that some of his contemporaries may not have recognized but for Machado it was much more the poet's vocation than the creation of 'new' visions of reality. This was made clear in his interview with Rivas-Cherif published in *La Internacional* in September 1920. Taking up an expression used by Valle-Inclán in replying to the question '¿Qué es el arte?', Machado notes that for some artists art is a kind of sport, 'juego libre o supremo juego'. But the poet opts for an art that is not superfluous to life, an unimportant pastime, but 'una actividad integral, de que son tributarias, en mayor o menor medida, todas las actividades del espíritu'. This explains why there is a tone of high seriousness in *Nuevas canciones*, as compared with the aesthetic games of *Ultra* or even the early works of Alberti and Lorca if we think of *jeux d'esprit* such as the 'Sonetos alejandrinos' of *Marinero en tierra* or the 'Seis caprichos' of *Poema del cante jondo*. Poetry thus becomes a creative task in a sense very different from that envisaged by Huidobro or Reverdy. 'De aquí surge un deber primordial para el artista, que consiste en mirar, no tanto al arte realizado como a las otras ramas de la cultura, y, sobre todo, a la naturaleza y a la vida' (*Poesía y prosa*, III, p. 1614). We note that culture, nature, and life are the raw materials. For Machado there were two different forms of artist: those who were genuinely creative, like bees who fly to the flowers to make honey; others, less creatively, feed off the half distilled products. He quotes the *copla*

> Si vino la primavera,
> volad a las flores;
> no chupéis cera.

which would become XVI of the 'Proverbios y cantares' in *Nuevas canciones* (*PP*, 629). As in the line 'No aséis lo que está cocido', Machado distinguishes between the artist who draws on nature, life and popular culture, and the 'neobarroquismo' of the young poets. Thus, when Rivas Cherif enquired '¿Qué debemos hacer?' it was clear that Machado would align himself with the genuinely creative poets to 'hacer arte de lo que todavía no lo es'. Challenging Valle he defends those poets who in times of crisis and hunger still find inspiration in nature, but he sees poetic material in 'los nuevos anhelos que agitan hoy el corazón del pueblo' (*Poesía y prosa*, III, p. 1616). It is clear, I think, that Machado construed these 'anhelos' in a very wide sense - wider than that found in 'Olivo del camino':

> Yo, por ahora, no hago más que Folklore, *autofolklore o folklore de mí mismo*. Mi próximo libro será, en gran parte, de coplas que no pretenden imitar la manera popular - inimitable e insuperable, aunque otra cosa piensen los maestros de retórica - sino coplas donde se contiene cuanto hay en mí de común con el alma que canta y piensa en el pueblo. Así creo yo continuar mi camino, sin cambiar de rumbo. (*Poesía y prosa*, III, p. 1616)[30]

Tuñón de Lara and Valverde are surely right to underline the significance of the interview with Rivas Cherif. Not only does Machado take the opportunity to provide his own definition of *creacionismo* and of that *naturaleza* that the poet refines,[31] but he also sets out both the general lines of his neopopularism (which was clearly different in respect of content from that of Alberti, Lorca and Diego) and the framework of *Nuevas canciones*, four years prior to its publication. It thus becomes of some importance to consider the nature of Machado's approach to *poesía tradicional*.

As was noted earlier, the importance to Machado of traditional verse, folksong and folklore hardly needs restating. He was the great-nephew of Agustín Durán and the son of Antonio Machado y Álvarez, 'Demófilo', the leading light together with Rodríguez Marín of the Folklore Society of Seville and virtually the founding father of folkore studies in Spain.[32] We no doubt underestimate the significance of the folksong movement among poets and scholars in Spain. Francis Newton referring to the similarity of development of the blues and of *cante jondo* noted:

> Thanks to the respect of progressive Spanish poets and folklorists for the common people, its early history is much better known than that of the blues. 'Demófilo' - the great folklorist and father of poets, Antonio Machado y Álvarez - published the first sketch of its evolution and collection of its verses in the 1880s. His pseudonym 'friend of the people' indicates the spirit in which Spanish intellectuals approach their subject.[33]

What seems clear, however, is that we need to see why such an interest becomes more marked and central in Machado in the period covered by the first edition of *Nuevas canciones*.

There was no lack of material available for Machado to further his interest in this area. Throughout the nineteenth century collectors such as Lafuente y Alcántara, Demófilo and Rodríguez Marín had copied much of the extant oral tradition.[34] In 1890 Barbieri's edition of the *Cancionero musical de Palacio* led the way for the investigation of the old songbooks, for the research of Menéndez Pidal and his team and for the extraordinarily influential *Versificación irregular en la poesía castellana* of Henríquez Ureña and Cejador's *La verdadera poesía castellana*.[35] Tejada and Alvar are clearly right to emphasize the significance of the latter; a high proportion of the poems copied in the anthology of traditional poets in *Los complementarios* are found in Cejador, as Alvar's detective work has demonstrated.[36]

It is to Alvar that we owe a further suggestive hypothesis. He notes that the first five poems of the series 'Canciones del Alto Duero' from *Nuevas canciones*, although this series does not appear in the 1924 edition of *Nuevas canciones*, are to be found in *Los complementarios* dated 1 April 1916, just over a fortnight after the poem 'En el tiempo' in which he remembered his father for the first time in many years. For Alvar this is profoundly significant:

> Antonio Machado gustó de la poesía tradicional, folklórica o popular; era una inclinación que pudo aprender en los trabajos familiares o en el espíritu de la Institución. Cuando en 1916 incorpora a su propio quehacer esta veta popular, compone 'Canciones del Alto Duero', y las compone por los mismos días que el recuerdo paterno le hizo escribir el emocionado poema que tituló 'En el tiempo'.[37]

Thus over the next few years, as Alvar points out, Machado was compiling *Nuevas canciones (1917-1920)*, his *autofolklore*, while Menéndez Pidal and Cejador produced their conflicting, and notably virulent, interpretations of the phenomenon. Inspired by the memory of his father, he refined the aesthetic of 'Los cantos de los niños', found in it a response to the challenge of *creacionismo* and found himself in sympathy with the neopopularists of the 1927 Generation. Machado, then, came to folk-poetry by a different route from Lorca, though perhaps with similar results, and by a markedly different route from Alberti, whose early verse, as he cheerfully confessed, had little to do with the *pueblo*. Even so, the 1924 edition of *Nuevas canciones* constitutes a significant contribution to that neopopularism which was for Alberti the true avant-garde in the early nineteen twenties.

This helps to counterbalance the negative view sustained by Dámaso Alonso in his essay 'Fanales de Antonio Machado', included in *Cuatro poetas españoles* (Madrid: Gredos, 1962). Alonso dismisses *Nuevas canciones* as 'un muestrario' (p. 149), attacks the meditative verse as displaying the harmful effects of philosophy and generally argues that little of value was published by Machado after the 1912 edition of *Campos de Castilla*. Some of Alonso's arguments bear little scrutiny. He finds in *Nuevas canciones* a lack of the structural unity he claims to discern in *Soledades, galerías y otros poemas* - whose final section, of course, is entitled 'Varia', suggesting if anything a lack of unity. For Machado the unity of inspiration in *Nuevas canciones* lay in the *auto-foklore*, the response of the poetic self to the poetic material that he described in the interview with Rivas Cherif, namely 'las otras ramas de la cultura, y, sobre todo... la naturaleza y... la vida' (*Poesía y prosa*, III, p. 1614). Thus even the apparently anomalous sonnet portraits of Baroja, Azorín and Pérez de Ayala would be seen to have their place. More significantly, Alonso's criticism simply ignores the tradition of meditative *coplas* that form so substantial a part of the collections of Lafuente y Alcántara and Rodríguez Marín. (Alonso himself in the early nineteen twenties was much more interested in the traditional songs of Gil Vicente than in the living tradition.)

From the above discussion two conclusions suggest themselves. First, despite Machado's somewhat nineteenth-century view of traditional verse, *Nuevas canciones (1917-1920)* can be seen as a work that was far less removed from the concerns and aesthetics of the young poets than might be supposed from the standard accounts of the topic. Second, it is a book that corresponds very precisely to what Machado had predicted in 1920, namely 'folklore de mí mismo'.

Works of art have the right to be read in their integrity. It is not being argued that *Nuevas canciones* is a forgotten masterpiece as tight-knit in its unity as, let us say, Guillén's *Cántico*. But neither is it a rag-bag of odds and ends. On the contrary, it seems to be a work that does not look at all out of place alongside Lorca's *Libro de poemas*, Diego's *Versos humanos* or the 1925 edition of Alberti's *Marinero en tierra*, both in its lay-out and in the

111

variety of form and poetic strategy. Certainly it has been argued that the opening poem 'Olivo del camino' is a declamatory piece like 'España en paz' and therefore equally to be dismissed. Yet, as we have seen, it corresponds to a persistent note in Machado's thought in the period between 1919 and 1922. The three sections 'Apuntes', 'Galerías' and 'Canciones de tierras altas' form a neat triptych that encapsulates the manner of the *neopopularismo* of the early twenties. 'Apuntes' with its series 'Tierra de olivar' and 'Hacia tierra baja' looks south, to Baeza and Western Andalusia respectively. 'Canciones de tierras altas' looks north, with its memories of Soria and Leonor. Set between them 'Galerías', the 'Apuntes para un estereoscopio vano' and 'La luna, la sombra y el bufón', is perhaps the climax of *autofolklore* proceeding from the landscape of foreboding to the picture of a barren world in a manner surprisingly similar to some of the more introverted verse of Diego and Lorca from that period. Both the 'Apuntes...' and 'La luna, la sombra y el bufón' perhaps follow the same path: in the one the world is 'vacío, ciego, alalo'; (*PP*, 615); in the second, the buffoon of a poet is impotent before Lucila's open balcony.[38] Significantly, the final - and most varied - section in the 1924 text is entitled 'Folklore'. It opens with the two sides of *poesía tradicional* as conventionally understood: the series 'Canciones de varias tierras' first published in *Los Lunes del Imparcial* in 1920; and the group of 'Proverbios y cantares' originally published in *Revista de Occidente*, the knotty sententiae that so puzzle some later commentators but which seem familiar in tone to those who know the great nineteenth-century collections of 'philosophical' *coplas*. Such a tone is also found in 'Parergón' with lines at once reminiscent of Juan Ramón and Campoamor:

> ¿cómo eran - preguntó - pardos o negros,
> sus ojos? ¿Glaucos? ...¿Grises?
> ¿Cómo eran, ¡Santo Dios!, que no recuerdo?... (*PP*, 647)

The references to the mysterious woman in Baeza, 'la enjauladita', link the little verses of 'Parergón' to 'Glosando a Ronsard'. This is where we encounter some occasional pieces, recalling the 'Elogios' of *Campos de Castilla*, alongside the splendidly tough sonnets of 'Los sueños dialogados' and the closing aesthetic statements of 'De mi cartera'. It is the sonnets, both 'Glosando a Ronsard' and 'Los sueños dialogados' that depict the poet's perplexity as new or potential love experiences come to him. For Sánchez Barbudo they are reminiscences of *Soledades*.[39] Yet they seem genuinely new in form and content for Machado.

Like the 'Proverbios y cantares' which anticipate the *Apócrifos*, these sonnets clearly look forward to the Guiomar series. On the other hand the book is rounded off by 'De mi cartera (Apuntes de 1902)', clearly serving as a résumé of Machado's critique of one side of the new poetry.

Toda la imaginería
que no ha brotado del río,
barata bisutería. (*PP*, 664)

In his reference to 1902 the poet implies his sense of having been consistent in his aesthetic from the time of *Soledades* and 'Los cantos de los niños'.

The sonnets and 'De mi cartera (Apuntes de 1902)' seem to exemplify the importance and the essential character of *Nuevas canciones (1917-1920)*. Rather than a drying up of the muse it charts the way ahead while, paradoxocially, briefly bringing Machado in some respects as near to poets such as Alberti and Lorca as was Juan Ramón. Not until the political *engagement* of the Second Republic were they to be so near again.

NOTES

1   Gerardo Diego, *Imagen. Poemas (1918-1921)* (Madrid: Gráfica Ambos Mundos, 1922), p. 9.

2   Rafael Alberti, *La arboleda perdida* (Buenos Aires: Fabril, p. 168). The new formalism was the subject of commentary at the time. Gerardo Diego, 'Retórica y poesía', *Revista de Occidente*, 6, no. 17 (November 1924), 286-87, claimed: 'Nos hallamos en los albores de una nueva edad - ¿siglo? ¿cincuentena? - de oro, de un fecundo y seguro de sí clasicismo.'

3   *Revista de Occidente*, 1, no. 11, 118.

4   Enrique Díez-Canedo, 'Antonio Machado, poeta japonés', *El Sol*, 20 June 1924, reprinted in *Antonio Machado* (El Escritor y la Crítica), edited by R. Gullón and A.W. Phillips (Madrid: Taurus, 1973), 361-63.

5   *Revista de Occidente*, 4, no. 12, 392-96.

6   In *Los complementarios* Machado contested this point citing 'Los cantos de los niños' from *Soledades*. *Poesía y prosa*, III, p. 1207.

7   José María Castellet, *Un cuarto de siglo de poesía española* (Barcelona: Seix Barral, 1964), p. 57.

8   Rafael Cansinos-Asséns, '*Nuevas canciones*', *El Imparcial*, 10 August 1924, reprinted in Gullón and Phillips, *Antonio Machado*, pp. 355-59. For Cansinos as the leading guru of *Ultra* see Gloria Videla, *El ultraísmo* (Madrid: Gredos, 1963). His unjustly neglected work on traditional verse has been collected in *La copla andaluza. Folclore*, Biblioteca de la Cultura Andaluza 11 (Granada: Editoriales Andaluzas Unidas, 1985).

9   *Antonio Machado y Baeza: a través de la crítica*, ed. Antonio Chicharro (Universidad de Verano de Baeza, 1983), p. 53.

10   Ian Gibson, *Federico García Lorca*, Volume 1, *De Fuente Vaqueros a Nueva York (1898-1929)* (Barcelona: Grijalbo, 1985), pp. 155, 162. For Lorca's intention to visit Machado in 1918 and Machado's personal interest in Lorca's work, see p. 190.

11   Pablo de A. Cobos, *Antonio Machado en Segovia*. *Vida y obra* (Madrid: Insula, 1973), pp. 89-90. Mariano Quintanilla, 'Antonio Machado en mi recuerdo', *Ínsula*, no. 262 (September 1968), 3, lists the visitors as Mauricio Bacarisse, Salinas, Ardavín, Chabás and Romero Flores.

12   *Poesía y prosa*, III, seems not to include the short article 'La carta de un poeta' which is reprinted in *Antonio Machado*. *Antología de su prosa*, ed. Aurora de Albornoz, Volume II, *Literatura y arte* (Madrid: EDICUSA, 1970), p. 113. It was published in *La Voz de Soria*, 8 September 1922. See A. Gallego Morell, *Vida y poesía de Gerardo Diego* (Barcelona: Aedos, 1956), p. 256.

13   Andrew P. Debicki, *Estudios sobre poesía española contemporánea* (Madrid: Gredos, 1968), pp. 262-84.

14   Alberti, *La arboleda perdida*, p. 158.

15   Rafael Alberti, *Imagen primera de...* (Madrid: Turner, 1975), p. 41.

16   Alberti, *La arboleda perdida*, p. 179.

17   Alberti, *La arboleda perdida*, pp. 202, 206.

18   Alberti, *Imagen primera de*, pp. 46-47.

19   John G. Cummins, *The Spanish Traditional Lyric* (Oxford: Pergamon, 1977), p. 163.

20   *Cartas de Antonio Machado a Juan Ramón Jiménez*, ed. Ricardo Gullón (Universidad de Puerto Rico, 1959), p. 62. The use of the phrase is curious: from *Unidad* (1925) it is none the less dated 1919, six years before the publication of *Marinero en tierra*.

21   Luis Cernuda's suggestion that Machado 'echoed' Alberti's *canciones* is quite properly dismissed by A. Sánchez Barbudo *Los poemas de Antonio Machado* (Barcelona: Lumen, 1967), pp. 348-49. Some of the Cadiz Bay poems were written by Machado in 1916 when he attended his brother's wedding in Puerto de Santa María. At that time Alberti was still a schoolboy.

22   Pedro Salinas, *Literatura española*. *Siglo XX* (Mexico: Séneca 1941), p. 221; Gabriel Pradal-Rodríguez, 'Vida y obra' in *Antonio Machado (1875-1939)* (New York: Hispanic Institute, 1951), p. 49; José María Valverde, 'Introducción' to Machado, *Nuevas canciones*. *Cancionero apócrifo*, Clásicos Castalia 32 (Madrid: Castalia, 1971), p. 39; Bernard Sesé, *Antonio Machado 1875-1939*. *El hombre. El poeta. El pensador*, 2 vols. (Madrid: Gredos, 1980), II, pp. 456-77.

23   Sesé, *Antonio Machado*, II, p. 468.

24   *Nuevas canciones (1917-1920)* (Madrid: Editorial Mundo Latino, 1924).

25   *Poesía y prosa*, III, pp. 1208-15. In *Los complementarios*, ed. Manuel Alvar (Madrid: Cátedra, 1980), p. 172, Machado includes the note: 'Vicente Huidobro: *Horizon carré* (Leída). Ecuatorial (id.) Poemas artísticos (pedir a Pueyo).' The latter was of course Huidobro's *Poemas árticos*.

26   The preliminary note to *Horizon carré*, quoted by David Bary, *Huidobro o la vocación poética* (Universidad de Granada, 1963), p. 53.

27   José María Valverde, *Antonio Machado* (Madrid: Siglo Veintiuno, 1978), pp. 54-60. More recently, Carlos Beceiro, '"Los cantos de los niños" de *Soledades* a *Soledades, galerías y otros poemas'*, *Insula*, nos. 506-07 (February-March 1989), 12-14, sees 'Los cantos de los niños' as a kind of poetic manifesto.

28   Vicente Huidobro, *Obras completas*, 2 vols. (Santiago de Chile: Zig-zag, 1964), I, 285-86.

29   Borges, 'Ultraísmo', *Nosotros*, 39, no. 151 (Buenos Aires, 1921) 468, quoted by Videla, *Ultraísmo*, pp. 107-08.

30   Originally reprinted by Manuel Tuñón de Lara, 'Un texto de Don Antonio Machado', *BH*, 71 (1969), 312-17. The text predates by about one month Machado's letter to Diego quoted above.

31   Machado develops this point in 'Naturaleza y arte' published in *El Sol*, September 1920: 'El artista no copia la naturaleza; pero liba en ella' (*Poesía y prosa*, III, p. 1610).

32   All standard accounts of Machado's life grant emphasis to this side of his work, but see particularly P. de Carvalho Neto, *La influencia del folklore en Antonio Machado* (Madrid: Ediciones Demófilo, 1975). The publishers of this short volume take their name from the pseuydonym of Machado's father Antonio Machado y Álvarez.

33   Francis Newton, *The Jazz Scene* (Harmondsworth: Penguin Books, 1961), p. 37.

34   For a brief account of the rediscovery of the popular tradition see Gustav Siebenmann, *Los estilos poéticos en España desde 1900* (Madrid: Gredos, 1973). The most influential nineteenth-century collections are: Lafuente y Alcántara, *Cancionero popular* (Madrid: Bailly-Baillière, 1865); A. Machado y Álvarez, *Colección de cantes flamencos* (Seville: El Porvenir, 1881); F. Rodríguez Marín, *Cantos populares españoles* (Seville: F. Alvarez, 1882-83).

35   *Cancionero musical de Palacio*, ed. F. Asenjo Barbieri (Madrid: Academia de Bellas Artes de San Fernando, 1890). P. Henríquez Urena, *La versificación irregular en la poesía castellana* (Madrid: Revista de Filología Española, 1920); Julio Cejador, *La verdadera poesía castellana*, 5 vols. (Madrid: Revista de Archivos, 1921-24).

36   José Luis Tejada, *Rafael Alberti, entre la tradición y la vanguardia* (Madrid: Gredos, 1977); Manuel Alvar, 'Antonio Machado y la lírica de tipo tradicional' in *Homenaje a Machado. Reunión de Málaga de 1975* (Málaga: Diputación Provincial, 1980), pp. 151-70.

37   Alvar, 'Machado y la lírica de tipo tradicional', p. 167.

38   In the 1924 edition of *Nuevas canciones* the section 'Galerías' included both 'Apuntes para un estereoscopio vano' (not 'Apuntes para un esteoscopio lírico' as Valverde has it in his edition, p. 124), CLVI in the *Poesías completas*, and 'La luna, la sombra y el bufón', CLVII. The latter was published in *Los Lunes Del Imparcial* in October 1920; its content is oddly reminiscent of some of Diego's self-deflating poems from *Imagen*, e.g. 'Ahogo'.

39   Sánchez Barbudo, *Los poemas*, 419-24.

Guiomar: the Nostalgic Vision

D. GARETH WALTERS

University of Glasgow

Shortly after the fiftieth anniversary of Machado's death, the popular weekly *Semana* printed a lengthy article on the poet and Guiomar, prompted by Andrés Amorós's dramatization of their relationship as revealed in the poet's correspondence.[1] I cite this article - topical as it is - not to scorn it, as might seem *de rigueur* for an academic confronted by low-brow journalism, but, rather, to draw attention to what the Guiomar phenomenon has represented not only for journalists but for academics themselves. In brief, we are confronting a modern myth that follows in the line of Petrarch and Laura or Garcilaso and Isabel Freire. Unfortunately, it is a myth in which the poetry does not figure very prominently. The years of silence about the identity of Guiomar and the embarrassed speculation about the nature of the relationship have inevitably fuelled interest in the person behind the name rather than the name within the text. And this priority has been detrimental to the work of art. The paucity of studies on Machado's Guiomar poems bears witness to critical inhibition. Moreover, those few commentators who have ventured into the poetry have fallen victim to an obligation to regard it as an appendage to the love-story and thus essentially anecdotal in character. Both Sánchez Barbudo and José María Valverde express dissatisfaction with the *Canciones a Guiomar* : they come away from the work, irritated that the boundary between real events and symbolism is not clearer. Bemoaning the lack of clarity in the composition, Valverde's conclusion is unequivocally dismissive:

> En conjunto, el poema es algo hermético y enigmático: el lector echa de menos las informaciones concretas que le permitan seguir el sentido del poema, su tema, sin quedarse fuera. Por eso, quizá sea uno de los menos afortunados de toda la obra de Antonio Machado, por su tono sibilino y por su imaginería de sueño, carentes de la clave necesaria.[2]

Likewise, Sánchez Barbudo is uneasy with the incorporation of biographical elements, in particular in the case of the third poem with its reference to the lovers' escape by train. After stating that 'los versos en general son más bien pobres', Sánchez Barbudo reveals how bogged down he is by a desire to verify the literal truth of what is described:

116

No sabemos que huyeran ellos a ninguna parte. Si hicieron algún viaje en tren juntos, lo más probable es que éste fuera tan solo de Segovia a Madrid. Pero no lo sabemos, claro, con certeza. En todo caso, en mi opinión, ésta es la peor de las "canciones" primeras a Guiomar.[3]

Somehow, then, the poems do not match up to the expectations provoked by the myth with its subtle blend of the real and the imagined. I also suspect that a contributory factor in the muted reception of the *Canciones a Guiomar* is their very style. Those who prefer an artist's work to betray a consistent development may well be disappointed by the apparent recidivism of this collection. Since the later poems of *Campos de Castilla*, Machado had evolved a mode of expression that tended to the concise, indeed the cryptic. Although Machado was never a slave to fashion, there is more than a trace of minimalism and neo-classical purity about the poetry he wrote in the decade preceding the publication of the *Canciones a Guiomar*, a decade which saw such similarly-styled works as Lorca's *Canciones*, Cernuda's *Perfil del aire* and the first compositions of Guillén's *Cántico*. Again, Machado flirts with surrealism in *Recuerdos de sueño, fiebre y duermivela* at the same time as his younger contemporaries were interesting themselves in that movement. It is from this same period - 1928-29 - that the *Canciones a Guiomar* date. We may well feel a block against compositions that take us back to the world of the earliest poetry - of *Soledades* especially - with its restricted and delicate symbolism, its stylized backdrop and its adoption of what could be termed a rhapsodical-whimsical tone. These poems differ also from the later set to Guiomar - first published in 1936 - the *Otras canciones*, in which the detached, ironic approach that we had come to expect from the apocryphal poetry is evident. Significantly, the *Otras canciones* are subtitled 'A la manera de Abel Martín y Juan de Mairena' - Machado's heteronyms - while the earlier collection bears no such indication. The later set has received greater attention and praise, mainly because it serves to illustrate the philosophy and ideas of Martín and Mairena rather than because of any greater poetic merit.

One important difference between the two collections to Guiomar resides in the very concept of the two works. The *Otras canciones* comprise a set of eight separate poems, the majority of which are brief, even cryptic, utterances. The earlier composition is, however, best viewed as a single poem divided into three sections; the failure of critics to acknowledge this essential unity does, I believe, lead them to mistakenly harsh criticism of the individual parts or what they consider to be individual poems.[4] But the *Canciones a Guiomar* satisfy three conditions for being considered a single work. In the first place, none of the three sections could convincingly exist independently of the others. While certain of the shorter poems in *Otras canciones a Guiomar* do run together, this is the product of their brevity and superficial similarity rather than of cogent development. Secondly, the *Canciones a Guiomar* would be damaged by the removal of any of its parts; this is certainly not the case with the later composition. Thirdly, the *Canciones a Guiomar* would not permit reconstruction: each of its parts fulfills its function in the place it is located. But, apart from the last two poems of *Otras canciones*, which form a culmination to the set, it would be possible to perform several changes of order, for example, the third and fourth poems could appear in reverse order (*PP*, 731). They are linked by references to a lady with a fan and to the notion of oblivion, but neither has an obvious precedence.

Let us now examine the individual parts of the *Canciones a Guiomar* in more detail. The poem falls into three sections, the last two of which are further sub-divided into two parts. In the case of the second section this division - conventionally indicated by asterisks - has the effect of isolating a mere five lines. The separation in the final section creates a more balanced distribution, however, so much so that Sánchez Barbudo interprets this division as a boundary between two separate poems and thus sees the line 'Hoy te escribo en mi celda de viajero' (l. 77) as ushering in a separate poem.

For the moment let us think of the work in such a way. At the start of each of the four parts are verbs that clearly denote mental activity. Doubt is expressed at the beginning of the poem ('No sabía'); in the second section, it is dreaming ('he soñado'); in the third, meditation ('Tu poeta piensa en ti'); and in the fourth, creativity or self-expression ('Hoy te escribo'). Moreover, each of these verbs generates within the respective sections, sooner or later, a related or developing mood. Thus, doubt unfolds in a series of questions in the form of alternatives; the dream concludes with a fanciful encomium; meditation leads to fantasy; and, finally, the creative intent aptly yields a fusion, a final synthesis. Furthermore, the organization of this material reveals symmetrical as well as organic traits. The first section, characterized entirely by doubt and questioning, finds its counterpart in the serene resolutions at the end of the poem. What we may then define as the central portion - the second and third parts (if we momentarily think of the work in terms of a four-fold division) - is made up of two complementary, not contrasting, sections. These clearly stand apart from the opening and concluding sections; they occupy different emotional territory and involve a distinct approach. As a dream and a fantasy respectively they suggest evasion, as shown in the quest for oblivion in section two - 'el doble cuento olvidamos' (l. 36) - and the desire for escape in the fantastic train-journey of the first part of the third section.

The work thus possesses a chiasmic design - ABBA - where the second A is in the nature of a resolution of the first. In that the poem *qua* construct articulates conflict and resolution and incorporates such features as development and variation within a framework of three (or is it four?) 'movements' we could say that it has a symphonic structure. This, of course, is not to ascribe to it any overt musical intent; it is, rather, to suggest by the analogy how taut and disciplined is the integration of the rational-emotional and semantico-structural components.

Let us pursue this line of inquiry a little further by examining in isolation the first and last parts. The contrast between them is evident in the very nuts and bolts of language: in syntax and morphology. The repeated questions of section one are matched - in a sense, answered - by the repeated exclamations of the final section. The alternatives of the first part are replaced by the co-ordinates of the last: compare the frequency of 'o' and 'y' in the respective sections. A view of experience that depends on exclusion gives way to one that is rooted in synthesis - in the inclusiveness of emotions and responses. This shift is too obvious to require extensive quotation; I would merely draw attention to the semantic evidence of the closing lines: the repetition of 'todo', the verb 'fundirse', the phrase 'una sola melodía', the harmonious implication of 'un coro de tardes y de auroras', and another reconciliation of opposites in the phrase 'el hoy de ayer'.

Thus far, we have established that we are dealing with a single poem of symmetrical as well as logical construction that contains a marked tendency to form contrasts. This last point begs a further question, that will lead us directly into the very material of the poem: what does the transformation within the poem bespeak, and not only *why* but *where* does it occur?

The first impression we have of the *Canciones a Guiomar* - perhaps from an inattentive reading - is one that we might glean from the closing lines. The final phrase - 'esta nostalgia mía' - is preceded by lines of mellow radiance that serve as the culmination of the mood of lushness, even self-indulgence, in the work. One takes leave of the work with a sense of well-being, tinged with melancholy, rather as after a hearing of Strauss's *Four Last Songs*. But this is merely to suggest the *mood* of nostalgia: a precise, if distant, recollection, allied to the vague but immediate longing of one who has not yet learnt to abandon dreams; it is another, more difficult, task to define and locate the *significance* of nostalgia in the work.

Such sweetness as the composition possesses contributes to the somewhat dated feel to which I referred above. Let us specify the sources . The first two sections (notice that another structural pattern is being observed) present us with a succession of images and ideas that hark back to the earliest published poetry of Machado. I refer to words such as 'limón', 'huerta', 'tarde', 'jardín' and 'fuente', and to the concepts of fruitfulness and barrenness, of absence and lethergy. Indeed the atmosphere in the first section, in particular, is nearly akin to that of the poetry of the younger Machado: it implies a limited, sad and insecure existence. This

119

section provides more than a passing resemblance to the very first poem of *Soledades*, 'El viajero':

> Está en la sala familiar, sombría,
> y entre nosotros, el querido hermano
> que en el sueño infantil de un claro día
> vimos partir hacia un país lejano. [...]
>   Deshójanse las copas otoñales
> del parque mustio y viejo.
> La tarde, tras los húmedos cristales,
> se pinta, y en el fondo del espejo.
>   El rostro del hermano se ilumina
> suavemente. ¿Floridos desengaños
> dorados por la tarde que declina?
> ¿Ansias de vida nueva en nuevos años?
> ¿Lamentará la juventud perdida?
> Lejos quedó - la pobre loba - muerta.
> ¿La blanca juventud nunca vivida
> teme, que ha de cantar ante su puerta?   (*PP*, 427)

Apart from the obvious lexical parallels ('claro día', 'tarde', 'espejo') we find, too, in 'El viajero' a persistent questioning that extends over the central stanzas of the poem. But, as I have stated above, the mood is not quite the same as in the Guiomar poem; with hindsight, we realize that while the questions in 'El viajero' are melancholic and musing, those in the *Canciones a Guiomar* have a latent energy: they are the seeds from which the work's harmonious conclusion will flower. But, for the moment, these questions will appear to be more redolent of anguish than of dynamic potential. Indeed, what follows - the second section and the first part of the third - constitutes a withdrawal in the face of the opening uncertainty.

In the secluded dream-setting of the second section, isolated in time as much as in space, the poet escapes the responsibility of the world of questions and of confrontations with reality. There, in safety, he can muse on fulfilment and frustration alike (the 'doble cuento') and thus aspire to oblivion.

The third section again is concerned initially with the world of the imagination. In his daydream, the poet's thoughts stray to the idea of flight, of escape with his goddess, the term also employed by Machado in later poems to Guiomar as well as in the letters. Such a yearning for fulfilment without responsibility offers a means of evasion, of postponing still further the need to face the questions - still unanswered from the first section. But within a few lines, we shall encounter synthesis, resolution, and even plenitude. We have arrived at the point of transition.

120

In the course of the fantasy-vision of escape at the start of the third section, Machado establishes a sub-text, a substratum of meaning through reminiscence that initially goes against the grain of the narrative. It is here that nostalgia, through poetic self-allusion, acquires a special significance. Hitherto, the reminiscences have been of *Soledades;* indeed, the opening lines of the third section continue in this vein:

> Tu poeta
>
> piensa en ti. La lejanía
> es de limón y violeta,
> verde el campo todavía. (ll. 48-51)

There immediately follows a description of the train journey - the fantasy-vision - which ushers in a series of allusions to *Campos de Castilla.* The sheer number of these is significant. Consequently, the first such reference - 'Conmigo vienes' - would not, in isolation, strike us as an echo of the brief refrain 'conmigo vais' from the second part of *Campos de Soria.* But in the context of succeeding reminiscences, such an association is plausible.

Before detailing these allusions, it is worth mentioning that the subject of the train journey figures prominently in *Campos de Castilla* as a location of and stimulus to composition, often of a reflective and introspective nature, as with the poem 'En tren' (*PP,* 509). Indeed, two such poems - 'Recuerdos' (*PP,* 542) and 'Otro viaje' (*PP,* 550) - are strongly imbued with memory. So much for the parallel of background. But the textual reminiscences function in a more complex fashion. Beneath the narrative layer that relates the poet's fantasy is a confrontation with a past event, recorded in a clearly-definable sub-grouping of poems from *Campos de Castilla.* For what we have from now until the end of the *Canciones a Guiomar* are several echoes of those poems inspired by the death of Leonor. Consider the following parallel. The quotation from the *Canciones a Guiomar* is printed first:

> Porque una diosa y su amante
> huyen juntos, jadeante,
> los sigue la luna llena. (ll. 60-62)

> La luna está subiendo
> amoratada, jadeante y llena. (*PP,* 545)

The lexical similarities are strikingly precise in these evocations of an ominous or malefic force. The next parallel involves an identical image with a similar symbolic resonance:

> Tras los montes de granito
> y otros montes de basalto,
> ya es la mar y el infinito. (ll. 66-68)

121

Tu voluntad se hizo, Señor, contra la mía.
Señor, ya estamos solos mi corazón y el mar. (*PP*, 546)

The sea image strikes us as more mysterious in the brief poem from *Campos de Castilla*, but in both instances it serves as a symbol of the unknown, of that which lies beyond.

In the second part of the third section (what Sánchez Barbudo regards as the fourth part in the work) we encounter further parallels. The phrase 'tarde niña' is interpreted by Valverde as the poet recalling his own and Guiomar's childhood.[5] But I would suggest another name. If we return to *Campos de Castilla*, we discover that 'niña' is how Leonor is described in the twenty-sixth poem of the collection - the fifth in the sub-group inspired by her death: 'tu voz de niña en mi oído' (547). Likewise, in the following poem, we read 'Mi niña quedó tranquila' (*PP*, 547). It is worth noting, too, how all the reminiscences from *Campos de Castilla* occur in the *Canciones a Guiomar* in the same order as in the earlier collection. Not surprisingly, the final echo comes from the next - and the last - poem in the group to Leonor. As the *Canciones a Guiomar* draws to a benedictory close, the poet invokes the image of 'esta luz de abril' (l. 89) as the propitious setting in which the synthesis is achieved, in which the opening conflicts and tensions are resolved. Similar in connotation is the reference to April at the start of the twenty-eighth poem of *Campos de Castilla*, the final one in the Leonor group:

Al borrarse la nieve, se alejaron
los montes de la sierra.
La vega ha verdecido
al sol de abril, la vega
tiene la verde llama,
la vida, que no pesa... (*PP*, 548)

This is a poem that is emotionally far removed from the despondency and bleakness of those two poems to which allusion was made in the course of the fantasy-vision. It expresses a strange hope, deriving consolation from an experience that is not so much mysterious as magical. In this connection, the final poem from the *Otras canciones a Guiomar* strikes a similar chord. This elusive and gnomic poem - a free sonnet - describes how a butterfly takes to flight, rising from a grave in which a rotting corpse sprouts roses. This transformation takes place, so the poet tells us, in the wonder-working light of May: 'que el sol de Mayo hechiza' (*PP*, 733).

No less miraculous in its way is the change that occurs in the *Canciones a Guiomar*. Parallel to the antithesis established between the opening and close of the work, but more condensed, urgent and emotionally-charged, is the implied antithesis achieved, as we have seen, by self-references not so much within as against the text.[6] For the fantasy-vision provoked simultaneous echoes of the harshest of realities: a re-engagement with loss and grief. But out of this, specifically, comes the final synthesis in the shape of the reconciliation of opposites. These lines contain a mingling of past and present, but there is also a union of loves as well as of times: of a past innocent love and a carnal love that is the poet's aspiration - an aspiration, not merely a dream as in the second section:

> ¡Y día adolescente
> - ojos claros y músculos morenos -,
> cuando pensaste a Amor, junto a la fuente,
> besar tus labios y apresar tus senos! (ll. 85-88)

Here also, from my reading of the poem, is the union of Leonor and Guiomar.[7]

This would be neither the first nor the last time that Machado would return to that area of experience involving the death of Leonor; those poems of desolation and nostalgia written in the year following his bereavement were not the last word on the subject. He returned to it musingly in 'Los sueños dialogados' from *Nuevas canciones*, and there are fleeting glimpses in the nightmarish vision of *Recuerdos de sueño, fiebre y duermivela*. The importance of the allusions to Leonor in the *Canciones a Guiomar* resides in the fact that here, as nowhere else, the experience is confronted and absorbed: there is an acceptance, as revealed in the entirely serene and harmonious conclusion - as convincing an integration as one could wish. The poet has progressed far from what Donald Shaw defines as a 'desperate hope' or what Sánchez Barbudo labels an 'irracional esperanza' - terms applicable to the Leonor poems in *Campos de Castilla*.[8] There the poet had sought consolation in a vaguely mystical apprehension of death, striking a note that sounds a trifle hollow. It was an attitude that, according to Shaw, had 'no deep roots in Machado's nature or upbringing'.[9] By contrast, the conclusion of the *Canciones a Guiomar* suggests a sober and profound assimilation of past experience.[10]

This analysis has been concerned neither with the identity of Guiomar nor with biographical matters except where these figure as inter-textual allusions. My discussion has focussed upon what Guiomar represents, not who she is: what the name involves and, to be specific, what the name invokes. For on each of its occurences in the work the name arises as an address, never as an occasion for a description of Guiomar or information about her. Indeed, two of these apostrophes reflect the emotional development and structural unity of the poem. Placed symmetrically and strategically at the end of the second section and in the last line of the composition respectively are two strikingly different addresses to Guiomar. The first of these takes the form of an extravagant eulogy; they are lines that have an unexpectedly gongoristic hue:

> Por ti la mar ensaya olas y espumas,
> y el iris, sobre el monte, otros colores,
> y el faisán de la aurora canto y plumas,
> y el búho de Minerva ojos mayores,
> Por ti, ¡oh Guiomar! ...　　　(ll. 44-48)

It is an appropriate location for such a grandiloquent gesture - between a dream and fantasy. If we bear in mind Machado's distaste for baroque literature, then this four-square encomium could be interpreted as a deliberately vapid tribute.[11] Such an interpretation is all the more likely when these lines are compared to the simple utterance at the work's end:

> A ti, Guiomar, esta nostalgia mía.　　　(l. 90)

There is a momentous change of register: the transformation embodied in the replacement of 'por ti' by 'a ti' epitomizes the sea-change that has happened in the intervening lines. In place of hyperbolic declaration we have a plain dedication or, better, an emotional donation. From being the source of conventional praise Guiomar has become both the source of reconciliation and, ultimately, the repository - the recipient - of the poet's confession.

NOTES

1　*Semana*, 1 March 1989, pp. 32-34. I am grateful to Margaret Tejerizo, Department of Slavonic Languages and Literatures, University of Glasgow, for drawing this article to my attention. Armand Baker wonders whether the letters are not 'una especie de diario poético que Machado haya escrito en forma epistolar' rather than letters in the accepted sense of the word. 'El ánima de Antonio Machado: análisis jungiano del tema de la amada en su obra', *Actas del Sexto Congreso Internacional de Hispanistas*, ed. Alan M. Gordon and Evelyn Rigg (Toronto: University of Toronto, 1980), 86.

2　Introduction to Antonio Machado, *Nuevas canciones y de un cancionero apócrifo* (Madrid: Castalia, 1971), p. 85.

3　A. Sánchez Barbudo, *Los poemas de Antonio Machado*, 2nd ed. (Barcelona: Lumen, 1969), p. 426.

4　For example, by seeing it as a poem in its own right Ricardo Navas-Ruiz views the first part of the work as incomplete: 'la respuesta no surge, la solución no aparece ... el poema no alcanza un clímax, psíquicamente no tiene fin'. 'Guiomar y el proceso creador de Antonio Machado', *Revista de literatura*, 69-70 (1969), 107.

5   Valverde, p. 251n.

6   Machado does not indulge widely in self-references. Ricardo Senabré draws attention to self-quotation in the the third of the four sonnets entitled 'Los sueños dialogados' whose opening line 'Las ascuas de un crepúsculo, señora' harks back to a poem in *Soledades*. 'Machado, entre Leonor y "Guiomar"', *Insula*, 344-45, p. 5. The kind of intertextual tension that is created by such a practice in the *Canciones a Guiomar*, however, is perhaps unique in the poet's work.

7   Navas Ruiz (p. 109) does not accept the possibility of this union of the two loves: 'Guiomar le ha sonreído, ofreciéndole aparentemente una invitación al amor. Pero, en su conciencia surge el recuerdo de otro gran amor, que aún conserva cálido: "solamente el recuerdo de mi mujer queda en mí, porque la muerte y la piedad lo han consagrado". Y al yuxtaponerse el presente y el pasado, éste tiñe aquél, creando la duda sin solución.' I would, however, commend Sebastián de la Nuez's conclusion on the late sonnet to Guiomar, 'De mar en mar': 'en estos años trágicos de lucha, de recuerdos de amor, de proximidad de la muerte, y junto a las evocaciones de Soria y de Segovia, surgirían ahora en el espíritu de Machado, y para siempre unidos ... los nombres de su niña y de su diosa, como llamó él, respectivamente, a Leonor y a Guiomar'. 'Amor y ausencia en unos poemas de Antonio Machado (De Leonor a Guiomar)', *Papeles de Son Armadans*, no. 249 (1980), 225-47 (247).

8   Donald L. Shaw, *The Generation of 1898 in Spain* (London: Ernest Benn, 1975), p. 138; Sánchez Barbudo, p. 254.

9   Shaw, p. 138.

10 It is tempting to draw a parallel with Garcilaso's treatment of the Nemoroso-Elisa relationship in his First and Third Eclogues. At the conclusion of the former, Nemoroso has a vision of Elisa in the after-life and anticipates reunion with her after death. This climax seems to me less convincing than the serene acceptance of death and the recognition of its place in the natural order of things, as is implied at the end of the Third Eclogue.

11 The negative view of the Spanish literary baroque is communicated principally via Juan de Mairena. He is at his most scathing when he writes of *culteranismo* and *conceptismo* in the following terms: 'la seca y árida tropología gongorina, arduo trasiego de imágenes genéricas, en el fondo puras definiciones ... un ejercicio de mera lógica, que sólo una crítica inepta o un gusto depravado puede confundir con la poesía' (*PP*, 701).

Machado and the Poetry of Cultural Memory

EDWARD F. STANTON

University of Kentucky

We have gathered to commemorate the fiftieth anniversary of Antonio Machado's death. I've had to think twice, three times before using the word 'commemorate'. We have not come here to *observe* an anniversary, because that suggests a punctilious performing of required ceremonies, and none of us is obligated to be here. Neither have we gathered to *celebrate*, since that implies acknowledging an occasion by festivity. If then we have come here to *commemorate*, we should ask what it is we are calling to remembrance or preserving in memory. As we all know (and I am afraid this may be particularly true in the Hispanic world), literary anniversaries are often occasions for rhetoric, for 'reevaluations' and rereadings which teach us more about the occasion than they do about the writer who is being honoured in the first place. We take from the author what best highlights our own interest, what we were working on anyhow - with or without the anniversary. A case in point was the celebration of Machado's centenary in 1975. (Spaniards had more than one reason for celebrating that year.) Some critics heralded a new age of ascendancy for Machado, when in fact his greatest influence on postwar Spanish literature had already run its course some five or ten years earlier.

I would like to believe there is a difference between the celebration of a writer's birth and the commemoration of his death, especially when that death was as pathetic and resonant as Machado's. It has been said before but it bears repeating today, that he died as much from Spain's tragedy as from an illness. The Civil War that had opened with one poet's death - García Lorca's - closed with another, less violent but just as poignant. And with that death a triple shroud fell: over the tired old body in Collioure, over the Second Republic, and over Spanish poetry, condemned to decades of exile, censorship, silence.

So I would like to begin by remembering Antonio Machado today, and by recalling his death almost exactly fifty years ago. Except that it was not early spring, at the beginning of Easter week, but the dead of winter, Ash Wednesday in fact, 3.30 in the afternoon. As the poet and critic Leopoldo de Luis noted, 'Aquel día debió de oscurecer muy pronto'.[1] Although death is rarely well written, Machado's had a poetic justice to it. In a hotel room in

126

the little fishing village on the French side of the border, his body was draped with a foreign flag, that of the Spanish Republic - the one Hemingway called the colour of blood, pus and permanganate. He was buried in a borrowed tomb, in a casket that had to be paid for by friends since the poet's family did not have enough money in hand.[2] As Julia Kristeva has said, a person of the twentieth century exists most honestly as a foreigner. Or in Machado's own words, much more humble, 'Todo nuestro vivir es emprestado. / Nada trajimos; nada llevaremos'.

Writing only a year after Machado's death (while he was an exile himself as a lecturer at the University of Glasgow), another poet from Seville, Luis Cernuda, said: 'Más que muerto, Machado parece ahora haber regresado a no sabemos qué patria suya real, que siempre estuvo añorando, mientras torpe y desmañado se arrinconaba contra la vida'.[3] On that day in Collioure, the truths of his life and work became one. He fulfilled the well-known prophecy of his own death with its metaphor of the sea: 'me encontraréis a bordo ligero de equipaje, / casi desnudo...' Come to think of it, the story of modern European art will record at least two events in Collioure, each with its *hijos de la mar*: Matisse and Derain painting their luminous seascapes in the summer of 1905, and Machado dying on that dark afternoon in the winter of 1939.

Another poet died an even more obscure death that winter, perhaps a month or two earlier. Not in a Mediterranean village but in a prison camp 'at the far end of the earth' as his widow put it, amid 'suffocating stench, filth, and typhus, lice, hunger and degradation, terror, armed guards, watchtowers and barbed wire'.[4] His emaciated body was not draped in a flag but stripped of its tattered clothing - even that couldn't be wasted. Nor was he buried in a borrowed casket and tomb but thrown into a common pit, a numbered tag on one of his legs.[5] And with him died, for the time being, some of the best Russian poetry of the twentieth century.

Osip Mandelstam was labelled an enemy of the people, and possession of his books became an offence punishable by law. His widow spent the next twenty years as an outcast, surviving the Great War (which obliterated personal loss even more than the Spanish conflict), fleeing from one town to another in the backwaters of the largest country on earth, hiding her husband's poems in a frying pan or committing them to memory when writing them on paper was too dangerous. In the words of another great poet, Anna Akhmatova, intimate friend of Osip and Nadezhda Mandelstam, this was the 'pre-Gutenberg epoch' in modern Russian literature when poems, stories and entire books were memorized to prevent their confiscation. The same went for certain ideas and ethical principles - everything that could survive in no other way.

Nadezhda Mandelstam was not alone in this undertaking but her case was unique. To begin with, her husband had been his country's best poet. Going over his words day and night, repeating the rhythms, tones and images peculiar to his voice, she was preserving for later generations some of the most original and brilliant verses ever written in the language. She also memorized poems by Akhmatova. The widow's fidelity to her husband's poems was rewarded by their being preserved and published abroad, where they won worldwide recognition by the mid-1960s.

The story would have ended there if Nadezhda Mandelstam had not decided to write her memoirs in the last years of her life. She had never been a writer. If she wrote anything before the two large volumes of her autobiography, it was only letters to friends or appeals to the Supreme Court. Yet when she finished her memoirs near the age of seventy, she had written a work that illuminated the consciousness of a nation. She was able to achieve this not only because of her moral stature as the widow of a martyred poet, but also because of another kind of prestige, one that was aesthetic, cultural: her mind and style had been formed by the language of her husband's verse, which had become her flesh through learning it by heart. Joseph Brodsky, one of the younger Russian poets who inherited Osip Mandelstam's legacy, has described the process in the way that is most fitting - poetically:

> And gradually those things grew on her. If there is any subsitute for love, it's memory. To memorize, then, is to restore intimacy. Gradually the lines of those poets became her mentality, became her identity. They supplied her not only with the plane of regard or angle of vision; more importantly, they became her linguistic norm. So when she set out to write her books, she was bound to gauge - by that time already unwittingly, instinctively - her sentences against theirs. The clarity and remorselessness of her pages, while reflecting the character of her mind, are also inevitable stylistic consequences of the poetry that had shaped that mind.[6]

What I would like to suggest is that the Mandelstam phenomenon in the postwar Soviet Union may cast an oblique light on the fate of Antonio Machado's poetry during the same years in Spain. I do this with some misgivings and fears since I am not a specialist in either poet's work, especially not Mandelstam's (I don't read Russian). My only consolation is that I will not resemble one of those thinkers Machado warned us against, 'que parecen estar siempre seguros de lo que dicen' (541).[7] I will speak trying to keep his words in mind: 'La inseguridad, la incertidumbre, la desconfianza, son acaso nuestras únicas verdades' (500).

My intention is not to compare and contrast Machado and Mandelstam except on the most primary level, in order to put them in context. It would be tempting for someone who knew both literatures well to compare the clarity, precision and concrete imagery espoused by

128

the Acmeists, of whom Mandelstam was the leading exponent, with what Machado modestly considered to be the greatest value of his poetry, and his generation's: 'la poda de ramas superfluas en el árbol de la lírica española' (46). Neither man was a political poet; Mandelstam might also have claimed 'mi verso brota de manantial sereno', without even bothering to mention the 'gotas de sangre jacobina' that coursed through Machado's veins. Mandelstam's poem against Stalin was exceptional in his work, like Machado's sonnet to the Republican General Lister. The Russian's poem cost him his life; Machado's, his posthumous reputation among the victors. As for the losers, he continued to be an ethical and poetic inspiration both inside and outside the country. For obvious reasons Machado was bedside reading for many exiled poets - 'los poetas del éxodo y el llanto' as León Felipe called them. But that is another story, less subtle, and one that has been told before.[8]

Luckily we also know the general lines of the story inside Spain, thanks largely to José Olivio Jiménez's sensitive book, *La presencia de Antonio Machado en la poesía española de posguerra*.[9] Without it I would not be able to explore what Unamuno might have called the *intrahistoria*, the inner history of Machado's work among the poets who stayed in the country. Following Brodsky's beautiful theory on the survival of Mandelstam's verse through memorization and its ultimate metamorphosis into prose, I believe that Machado's poetry consituted a kind of cultural memory among Spanish writers, *mutatis mutandis*, during the same historical period.

It is well known that Machado and Juan Ramón Jiménez were the most widely read, quoted and imitated poets of the period. But Don Antonio possessed an advantage over the ill-tempered Juan Ramón: his moral prestige as a man who had lived and suffered not only for his work but also for his ideals. In her preliminary remarks to an anthology of Machado's prose, Aurora de Albornoz says: 'Hay momentos en que los pueblos necesitan guías, maestros, hombres mejores, que hagan creer en algo. La juventud española... sintió vivamente la ausencia de hombres ejemplares. Con frecuencia tuvo que ir hacia atrás, hacia el pasado - pasado vivo, actual aún, y sangrante - para encontrarlos'.[10] Machado was the most exemplary man of all because he enjoyed ethical stature as a martyr of the war in addition to his artistic prestige as a poet. Just as Mandelstam had been both a victim of Stalin's purge as well as a great poet, José Bergamín recognized 'la doble ejemplaridad que ofrece la vida y la obra de Antonio Machado'. Following the same line of thought, Guillermo de Torre spoke of 'Poesía y ejemplo de Antonio Machado', and Leopoldo de Luis titled his book *Antonio Machado, ejemplo y lección*.[11]

What else made his poetry so attractive, so memorable? This is a difficult question, yet we are forced to attempt a reply: it bears closely on the way Machado's work was received by younger generations. I believe the answer lies above all in what Hugh Kenner recently called 'poetry's ancient mnemonic function'.[12] When a poet creates lines and we remember them, it is primarily their sound that moves in the mind, the fragile rhythm of accents and pauses, rises and falls in pitch. That is why Wordsworth shouted passages aloud before committing them to paper, why Ezra Pound composed by chanting nonsense syllables, and why Robert Frost claimed that the sound of poetry is like a conversation heard from the next room: a melody lacking words. 'The strong poem survives its sense', says Kenner. And Machado had an uncanny ability to craft verses whose melody echoes in our memory. He managed to reproduce the rhythms of speech within the meters of Spanish prosody, giving us an impression of inevitability:

> ... Y avancé en mi sueño
> por una larga, escueta galería,
> sintiendo el roce de la veste pura
> y el palpitar suave de la mano amiga.
>
> Y todo en la memoria se perdía
> como una pompa de jabón al viento.
>
> La vi un momento asomar
> en las torres del olvido.

These lines also demonstrate Machado's concision, what Geoffrey Ribbans has called his 'extraordinary power of concentration in single lines and sentences'. [13] Add to this the consistency of his poetic world with its constant repetition of key words - *tarde, sueño, piedra, fuente, agua, plaza, jardín, sombra, espejo, galería, camino, viento, sol, río, colina, álamo*; the concreteness of his images no matter how intangible their referents; finally the apparent simplicity of his lines - which make it seem that almost anybody could have written them -, and you have a rough formula for Machado as the most memorable poet in modern Spain.

Although an exhaustive study has never been made (it would take years), I would guess that more Spanish writers of our time have attested to knowing his lines by heart than any other poet's.[14] In this respect we could cite the words of Vicente Aleixandre. On the centenary in 1975, he confessed that Machado was the only Spaniard whose complete poems he had memorized: 'Sólo en la memoria fidelísima se han repetido como palabras sin fallo en el corazón sin olvido'.[15] Aleixandre's words reveal the privacy of his relation to Machado - 'sólo en la memoria fidelísima' - and its inner quality - 'en el corazón sin olvido'. (By the way, these words could have been pronounced by Nadezhda Mandelstam about her husband's poetry.)

Many Spaniards had secret love affairs with Antonio Machado's work after the Civil War. Provided they ignored his politics, they had access to his writings except for a few poems and quite a lot of prose, including everything he had written for the magazine *Hora de España* during the hostilities. Only a year after the war, Dionisio Ridruejo, still a member of the Falangist Party, spoke of 'rescuing' the poet from his wayward allegiance to the Republic.[16] Within the body of poetry that was not expurgated, the early, introspective *Soledades* and *Soledades, galerías y otros poemas* were generally preferred to the later, more controversial *Campos de Castilla* and *Nuevas canciones*. The man who confessed that he was 'siempre buscando a Dios entre la niebla', and who had affirmed that 'quien habla solo espera hablar a Dios un día', was an inspiration for the kind of subjective religious poetry that began to appear in the 1940s. One of the best of the younger poets, José María Valverde, declared himself a disciple of Machado, whom he called 'mi inagotable maestro'.[17] In fact he has dedicated so many poems, essays and books to his master that José Olivio Jiménez has suggested that we might switch the terms, calling Valverde Machado's 'inagotable discípulo'.[18] Valverde wrote in one of his poems:

> ... el rozar un poco la verdad
> en español y en verso, hace que suenen
> ecos de otra voz, siempre necesaria:
> la de Antonio Machado.[19]

Notice the image of the voice and its echoes, which will be repeated with variants by other poets, suggesting the intimacy of their relationship to Machado, as if he whispered to them across the years.

If young Spanish writers were attracted to Machado's earlier verse during the years immediately after the Civil War, by the 1950s a shift in taste occurred. The state of the country demanded change, and poetry could sometimes quicken the nation's conscience more easily than prose because it was censored with less rigour. The poets of the new generation also saw Machado as a model. In 1957 Cernuda observed: 'Hoy, cuando cualquier poeta trata de expresar su admiración hacia un poeta anterior, lo usual es que mencione el nombre de Antonio Machado'.[20] Rather than his introspective verse, the young poets were drawn to his mature work where the preoccupation with existential time gave way to an historical consciousness. His critical vision of a frivolous, backward Spain, expressed in poems like '...Coplas por la muerte de don Guido', 'Del pasado efímero' and 'El mañana efímero' in *Campos de Castilla*, had come to life in a whole social class under Franco.

> La España de charanga y pandereta,
> cerrado y sacristía,
> devota de Frascuelo y de María...

continued its devotion to the Virgin who it really believed had intervened on its side in the war, and worshipped a new generation of bullfighters that had begun with the great Manolete. What was even worse, this superficial, picturesque Spain was going to be packaged and sold to the highest bidder in the impending tourist boom. For a young poet or intellectual who saw what was happening to the country, Machado's work must have seemed like a secret dialogue between the past and present, as well as a hope for a different, truer Spain.

The best poet of this tendency and the one most immersed in Machado's writings was Blas de Otero, to whom Don Antonio seemed more like a friend than a master. Whether by chance or not, the trajectory of Otero's career repeated his predecessor's: a private voice of religious searching followed by a more public style addressed to 'la inmensa mayoría', and finally a powerful synthesis in some of the mature lyrics. Blas inherited Machado's critical attitude toward Spain; his poems also tend to move from a bitter present to a more hopeful future.[21] In 'No te aduermas' he says, for example:

> Oh derramada España
> rota guitarra vieja,
> levanta
> los párpados
> (canta
> un gallo) que viene,
> llena de vida,
> la madrugada.[22]

We cannot help but hear Machado's dusty old 'Guitarra del mesón' in these lines, and recall 'los gallos de la aurora' from his well-known poem to Azorín.[23] The older man's voice permeates this and many other pieces by Otero, both in their deep structure, probably unconscious, and in the more obvious echoes of specific images. As Machado said, 'Todo poema es, en cierto modo, un palimpsesto'.[24]

Machado's influence reached its peak around the late 1950s and early 1960s, when José María Castellet dedicated two key anthologies to his memory - *Veinte años de poesía española* and *Un cuarto de siglo de poesía española*. Discussing at length Machado's unfinished inaugural speech for the Royal Academy, Castellet saw it as a prophecy of the new spirit in Spanish poetry: 'Las palabras de Machado resuenan hoy, como profecía cumplida, en los versos de nuestros más jóvenes y mejores poetas... Su talla intelectual, su honestidad y el acierto de sus predicciones acerca del futuro de la poesía, le han situado como maestro indiscutible en los últimos años de la poesía española'.[25] We might recall an earlier anthology, Gerardo Diego's classic *Poesía española* (1931), where Machado had confessed his disagreement with the poets of 1927 and also had foreseen the development of Spanish poetry twenty-five years later: 'Muy de acuerdo, en cambio, con los poetas futuros de mi Antología, que daré a la estampa, cultivadores de una lírica, otra vez inmergida en las "mesmas aguas de la vida", dicho sea con frase de la pobre Teresa de Jesús' (49-50). One of the younger poets who might have been included in that personal anthology (as he was in Castellet's), José Angel Valente, addressed the following poem to the 'maestro indiscutible':

> Si supieras cómo ha quedado
> tu palabra profunda y grave
> prolongándose, resonando...
> Cómo se extiende contra la noche,
> contra el vacío o la mentira,
> su luz mayor sobre nosotros...
>
> Si supieras cómo acudimos
> a tu verdad, cómo a tu duda
> nos acercamos para hallarnos,
> para saber si entre los ecos
> hay una voz y hablar con ella.[26]

Again the writer feels Machado not as a distant influence but as a familiar voice that reverberates in his own lines.

By the late 1960s the winds of change were blowing again. The end of Spain's isolation from the international community, mass tourism, the relative prosperity of the times, and the loosening of censorship favoured a new kind of poetry. A generation of young writers, many of them born after the Civil War, now looked to the Generation of 1927 or to foreign authors for their inspiration, or even outside literature to the media, popular music and cinema. Again it was Castellet who sensed the new spirit and enshrined it in his 1970 anthology, *Nueve novísimos poetas españoles* (Barcelona: Seix Barral, 1970). Don Antonio, born a full century before, with his absolute lack of frivolity and his sober concern for the moral and metaphysical destiny of mankind, seemed a little old-fashioned to the young poets who went to the movies, watched television, read comic books, and listened to jazz or rock and roll. It was ironic that Machado's influence on writers was waning at the very time when his poetry was reaching an ever-larger audience through popular settings of his words to music, such as Joan Manuel Serrat's well-known recording. The poet himself did not like his verses to be read aloud: 'No están hechos para recitados', he once wrote in his notebooks, 'sino para que las palabras creen representaciones'.[27] He classified his own contribution to the Spanish lyric as 'intimismo': his poems were not made to be recited or sung, but to be repeated silently in the mind, to be memorized. In contrast, the verses of a writer like Lorca lent themselves more readily to being recited or set to music. If he is the most recited poet, Machado could be called the most memorized poet of modern Spain.

The history of the Spanish lyric in the twenty-five years after the Civil War was a recapitulation of Machado's own development from a subjective to a more objective voice, and finally toward an occasional fusion of both in his best later work. In prosperous, democratic Spain today, his poetry and prose can finally be read and appreciated as a whole without prejudice in favour of a single phase or aspect. The eclectic nature of postmodernist writing makes it difficult to gauge his influence among the latest generation of poets. With the death of ideology in our time, his social and political thought has clearly become less urgent than in the Franco years, although he has ironically become a semi-official poet of the ruling Socialist Workers' Party in Spain. The twilight of another century and the pendular swing of taste would seem to point to a greater interest in the youthful poetry written by Machado during the last *fin de siècle*. The present artistic climate of world-weariness, the sense that there is nothing new under the sun - 'todo ha sucedido ya' -, the new sentimentality and nostalgia might lead us to believe that younger writers are reading a lot of his early verse nowadays. But the evidence does not show this. The poet Angel González told me recently, 'En general, Machado es todavía un poeta mal leído: los más jóvenes tienden a ignorarlo. ¡Grave ignorancia!'[28]

Antonio Machado used to stop to distinguish live voices from mere echoes. After his death at the end of the Spanish Civil War, younger poets also stopped to listen, and those with a good ear reconized his voice as one of the most authentic and memorable. Like Mandelstam's, it vibrated with the dual resonance of art and morality. It gave the new poets a vision and a poetic norm. To memorize Machado was to restore intimacy with him and all he stood for. He grew on the younger poets, in them: 'en la memoria fidelísima... en el corazón sin olvido'. Gradually his words and his vision became theirs, part of their thought and their identity. That is why they felt so close to him, closer than to any other poet, and that is why his words came to their minds and to their lips when they began to speak with their own voices. He had become a part of their cultural memory. Once more poetry showed its ancient mnemonic power. As Machado put it: 'y la ola humilde a nuestros labios vino/de unas pocas palabras verdaderas'. And if we extended Brodsky's theory by speculating that Machado's verse, like Mandelstam's, was transformed into prose during the postwar years, I would not be surprised if we found echoes of his work in such key novels as Martín Santos' *Tiempo de silencio* and Goytisolo's *Señas de identidad*.[29]

We know that Machado's poems often progress from a sterile present to a more fruitful tomorrow, from criticism to affirmation: from the crucified Christ to the Jesus who walked on the sea, from the withered old elm tree to its rebirth by a miracle of spring. In the same way, I would like this paper, which began by recalling Machado's death, to end with an affirmation.

After all, we would not be here today if the poet's words were not still alive. And I would like to give the last word to another poet. Referring to Nadezhda Mandelstam's resurrection of her husband's voice, Brodsky says that her achievement was unchallengeable. Not, as we might think, because of the brutal dimension of her husband's suffering, and her own. 'It's an abominable fallacy that suffering makes for greater art', Brodsky says. He goes on: 'Suffering blinds, deafens, ruins, and often kills. Osip Mandelstam was a great poet *before* the Revolution. So was Anna Akhmatova... They would have become what they became even if none of the historical events that befell Russia in this century had taken place: because they were *gifted*'.[30] Machado was also gifted; of course he was a great poet *before* the Civil War, and he would have been read, memorized and assimilated no matter what historical events had occurred in Spain. 'Basically,' as Brodsky concludes, 'talent doesn't need history.'

NOTES

1   *Antonio Machado, ejemplo y lección* (Madrid: Sociedad General Española de Librería, 1975), p. 162.

2   Joaquín Gómez Burón, *Exilio y muerte de Antonio Machado.* (Madrid: Sedmay, 1975), pp. 159-60, 162.

3   'Antonio Machado y la actual generación de poetas', *BSS*, 17 (1940), 139-43 (139).

4   Nadezhda Mandelstam, *Hope Abandoned* (New York: Atheneum, 1974), p. 306.

5   N. Mandelstam, *Hope Against Hope. A Memoir* (New York: Atheneum, 1970), pp. 382-83.

6   'Nadezhda Mandelstam (1899-1980): An Obituary', in *Less Than One* (New York: Farrar Straus Giroux, 1986), pp. 145-56 (pp. 150-51).

7   Page numbers in parentheses refer to *A.M. Obras: poesía, prosa*, ed. Aurora de Albornoz and Guillermo de Torre (Buenos Aires, 1964).

8   See Aurora de Albornoz, *El exilio español de 1939*, Cultura y Literatura IV (Madrid: Taurus, 1977), and Manuel Andújar, 'Resonancias de Antonio Machado', *CHA*, 102 (1975), 913-19 (913).

9   Lincoln, Neb.: Society of Spanish and Spanish-American Studies, 1983.

1 0   *Antonio Machado, Antología de su prosa*, 2 vols. (Madrid: *Cuadernos para el Diálogo*, 1970), I, 15. Albornoz is referring to the 1950s and 1960s but we could say much the same of the 1940s.

1 1   José Bergamín, 'Antonio Machado, el bueno', *La Torre*, 12 (1964), 257-64 (261-62); De Torre, *La aventura estética de nuestra edad* (Barcelona: Seix Barral, 1962), pp. 288-310; Leopoldo de Luis's book is cited in note 1.

1 2 'Ear Culture', *Harper's Magazine*, 278 (March 1989), 26-27, 30 (26). The quote from Kenner below is on p. 27. The complete essay is published as 'Teaching Poetry' in *Teaching Literature. What is Needed Now*, ed. James Engell and David Perkins (Cambridge, Mass. and London: Harvard U.P., 1988), pp. 3-11.

1 3 *Antonio Machado (1875-1939). Poetry and Integrity* (Nineteenth Annual Canning House Lecture) (London: Hispanic and Luso Brazilian Council, 1975), p. 6.

1 4 Besides Aleixandre, cited in this paragraph, I recall Rafael Alberti, Vicente Gaos, Eladio Cabañero and Félix Grande who have said so in public. See Alberti, 'Imagen sucesiva de Antonio Machado', in *Antonio Machado*, ed. Ricardo Gullón and Allen W. Phillips (Madrid: Taurus, 1973), pp. 23-30 (p. 23); Gaos, 'Recuerdo de A.M.', Gullón and Phillips, pp. 47-51 (p. 48); Grande (speaking for himself and Cabañero), cited in Jiménez, *La presencia de Antonio Machado en la poesía española de posguerra* (hereafter abbreviated as Jiménez), pp. 189-90.

1 5 'Antonio Machado, un recuerdo', *Insula*, nos. 344-45 (July-August 1975), 1. Reprinted in *Estudios sobre Antonio Machado*, ed. by José Angeles (Barcelona: Ariel, 1977), pp. 19-20.

1 6 Introduction to *Poesías completas*, 5th ed. (Madrid: Espasa-Calpe, 1940).

1 7 In Francisco Ribes, *Antología consultada de la joven poesía española* (Santander: Bedia, 1952), p. 199.

1 8 Jiménez, p. 167.

1 9 'Homenaje a algunos buenos', in *Enseñanzas de la edad (Poesía 1945-1970)* (Barcelona: Barral, 1971), p. 205; cited in Jiménez, p. 168.

2 0 'Antonio Machado (1876-1939)', in *Estudios sobre poesía española contemporánea* (Madrid: Guadarrama, 1957), pp. 103-18 (p. 105).

2 1 Jiménez, p. 156

2 2 *Que trata de España* (Paris: Ruedo Ibérico, 1964), p. 95; cited in Jiménez, p. 102. Although this book was published in France, Otero makes the point that it was written 'dentro y fuera de esta patria' (p. 9).

2 3 Jiménez, p. 102; (*PP*, 594).

2 4 *Poesía y prosa*, III, p. 1314.

2 5 *Un cuarto de siglo de poesía española (1939-1964)* (Barcelona: Seix Barral, 1966), p. 64.

2 6 'Si supieras', originally published in *La memoria y los signos* (1966), reprinted in *Punto cero (Poesía 1953-1979)* (Barcelona: Seix Barral, 1980), pp. 214-16 (pp. 214-15); cited in Jiménez, p. 181.

2 7 *Poesía y prosa*, III, p. 1188.

2 8 Letter to author, 28 January 1989.

2 9 I owe this insight in large part to Prof. Derek Gagen, to whom I am grateful.

30 'N. Mandelstam (1899-1980)', *Less Than One*, p. 153. The final quotation from Brodsky is on the same page.